THE
KARMA
OF
QUESTIONS

Essays on the Buddhist Path

by

Thanissaro Bhikkhu
(Geoffrey DeGraff)

for free distribution

Contents

Introduction

There's no such thing as a totally idle question. Every question, even the most casual, carries an intention: the desire for an answer to fit a certain purpose. You might think of a question as a mold for a tool. The emptiness of the mold indicates the desired but missing knowledge; the shape of the mold, the use to which the knowledge will be put. Most people, when looking at a question, focus on the emptiness of the mold. The karma or power of the question, though, lies in its shape. If you ask "Where did the universe come from?", the answer can't be "jump." Any answer acceptable to the question has to address the ideas about existence, causality, and sources implicit in "universe," "come from," and "where." And whatever stance the answer takes with regard to those ideas, it has to fit into the mold provided by the question. Even if it were to state that there is no universe or that the universe didn't come from anywhere, the act of giving an answer would affirm that the mold shapes a useful tool: an idea important enough to merit talking about and taking a stance.

The danger here is that if your actual problem requires a screwdriver, but your questions are designed to mold a hammer, any answers that fill the mold may do more harm than good. If you don't abandon the mold, then even if you're given a screwdriver, you'll force it into the mold, add scraps of metal from here and there, and turn it into a hammer.

This was why the Buddha approached questions with great care. He divided them into four sorts: those deserving a straight answer, those that need their terms redefined, those deserving a counter-question in response, and those that should be put aside. In other words, he saw that some molds were useful as is, some needed adjusting, some were best countered with an alternative mold, and others were best thrown away. His criterion for classifying questions in this way was whether the answers would be useful in putting an end to suffering and stress.

As he had noted, suffering leads to two reactions: bewilderment ("Why is this happening to *me*?") and search ("Is there anyone who knows how to put an end to this pain?"). These two reactions are a potent combination. If handled unskillfully, bewilderment can turn into ignorance, and search into craving—a surefire recipe for even more suffering. But if framed into a skillful strategy of clear and thoughtful questions, they take you to total freedom, beyond aging and death. So he deliberately framed his teachings to answer only the right questions. And he was especially careful to avoid questions that would foster craving or ignorance, delaying or obstructing the ending of stress.

The essays in this book are an attempt to follow the Buddha's example in approaching questions, trying to trace back to the questions that molded his teachings, and resisting the temptation to focus on questions that would force those teachings into a different shape. I've gone on the assumption that his screwdrivers were so well-designed that they are right for our needs today, and that we should guard against turning them into hammers. If you find that the tools offered in this book are useful in ending your own sufferings, then I've succeeded in my task.

Some of these essays, in earlier incarnations, have appeared in *Tricycle, Buddhadharma, Inquiring Mind*, and *Insight Journal*. The fact that they were originally intended for different audiences explains the overlap that occasionally occurs among them. It also explains the inconsistent use of Sanskrit and Pali terms: *dharma, karma,* and *nirvana* in some essays; *dhamma, kamma,* and *nibbana* in others. I hope that this poses no difficulties.

Ṭhānissaro Bhikkhu
(Geoffrey DeGraff)

Metta Forest Monastery
Valley Center, CA 92082-1409
September, 2002

Life Isn't Just Suffering

"He showed me the brightness of the world."

That's how my teacher, Ajaan Fuang, once characterized his debt to *his* teacher, Ajaan Lee. His words took me by surprise. I had only recently come to study with him, still fresh from a school where I had learned that serious Buddhists took a negative, pessimistic view of the world. Yet here was a man who had given his life to the practice of the Buddha's teachings, speaking of the world's brightness. Of course, by "brightness" he wasn't referring to the joys of the arts, food, travel, sports, family life, or any of the other sections of the Sunday newspaper. He was talking about a deeper happiness that comes from within. As I came to know him, I gained a sense of how deeply happy he was. He may have been skeptical about a lot of human pretenses, but I would never describe him as negative or pessimistic. "Realistic" would be closer to the truth. Yet for a long time I couldn't shake the sense of paradox I felt over how the pessimism of the Buddhist texts could find embodiment in such a solidly happy person.

Only when I began to look directly at the early texts did I realize that what I thought was a paradox was actually an irony—the irony of how Buddhism, which gives such a positive view of a human being's potential for finding true happiness, could be branded in the West as negative and pessimistic.

You've probably heard the rumor that "Life is suffering" is Buddhism's first principle, the Buddha's first noble truth. It's a rumor with good credentials, spread by well-respected academics and Dharma teachers alike, but a rumor nonetheless. The truth about the noble truths is far more interesting. The Buddha taught four truths—not one—about life: There is suffering, there is a cause for suffering, there is an end of suffering, and there is a path of practice that puts an end to suffering. These truths, taken as a whole, are far from pessimistic. They're a practical, problem-solving approach—the way a doctor approaches an illness, or a mechanic a faulty engine. You identify a problem and look for its cause. You then put an end to the problem by eliminating the cause.

What's special about the Buddha's approach is that the problem he attacks is the whole of human suffering, and the solution he offers is something human beings can do for themselves. Just as a doctor with a surefire cure for measles isn't afraid of measles, the Buddha isn't afraid of any aspect of human suffering. And, having experienced a happiness totally unconditional, he's not afraid to point out the suffering and stress inherent in places where most of us would rather not see it—in the conditioned pleasures we cling to. He teaches us not to deny that suffering and stress or to run away from it, but to stand still and face up to it, to examine it carefully. That way—by understanding it—we can ferret out its cause and put an end to it. Totally. How confident can you get?

A fair number of writers have pointed out the basic confidence inherent in the four noble truths, and yet the rumor of Buddhism's pessimism persists. I wonder why. One possible explanation is that, in coming to Buddhism, we sub-consciously expect it to address issues that have a long history in our own culture. By starting out with suffering as his first truth, the Buddha seems to be offering his position on a question with a long history in the West: is the world basically good or bad?

According to Genesis, this was the first question that occurred to God after he had finished his creation: had he done a good job? He then looked at the world and saw that it was good. Ever since then, people in the West have sided with or against God on his answer, but in doing so they have affirmed that the question was worth asking to begin with. When Theravada—the only form of Buddhism to take on Christianity when Europe colonized Asia—was looking for ways to head off what it saw as the missionary menace, Buddhists who had received their education from the missionaries assumed that the question was valid and pressed the first noble truth into service as a refutation of the Christian God: look at how miserable life is, they said, and it's hard to accept God's verdict on his handiwork.

This debating strategy may have scored a few points at the time, and it's easy to find Buddhist apologists who—still living in the colonial past—keep trying to score the same points. The real issue, though, is whether the Buddha intended his first noble truth to answer God's question in the first place and—

more importantly—whether we're getting the most out of the first noble truth if we see it in that light.

It's hard to imagine what you could accomplish by saying that life is suffering. You'd have to spend your time arguing with people who see more than just suffering in life. The Buddha himself says as much in one of his discourses. A brahman named Long-nails (Dighanakha) comes to him and announces that he doesn't approve of anything. This would have been a perfect time for the Buddha, if he had wanted, to chime in with the truth that life is suffering. Instead, he attacks the whole notion of taking a stand on whether life is worthy of approval. There are three possible answers to this question, he says: (1) nothing is worthy of approval, (2) everything is, and (3) some things are and some things aren't. If you take any of these three positions, you end up arguing with the people who take either of the other two positions. And where does that get you?

The Buddha then teaches Long-nails to look at his body and feelings as instances of the first noble truth: they're stressful, inconstant, and don't deserve to be clung to as self. Long-nails follows the Buddha's instructions and, in letting go of his attachment to body and feelings, gains his first glimpse of the Deathless, of what it's like to be totally free from suffering.

The point of this story is that trying to answer God's question, passing judgment on the world, is a waste of time. And it offers a better use for the first noble truth: looking at things, not in terms of "world" or "life," but simply identifying suffering so that you can comprehend it, let it go, and attain release. Rather than asking us to make a blanket judgment—which, in effect, would be asking us to be blind partisans—the first noble truth asks us to look and see precisely where the problem of suffering lies.

Other discourses show that the problem isn't with body and feelings in and of themselves. They themselves aren't suffering. The suffering lies in clinging to them. In his definition of the first noble truth, the Buddha summarizes all types of suffering under the phrase, "the five aggregates of clinging": clinging to physical form (including the body), feelings, perceptions, thought constructs, and consciousness. However, when the five aggregates are free from clinging, he tells us, they lead to long-term benefit and happiness.

So the first noble truth, simply put, is that *clinging* is suffering. It's because of clinging that physical pain becomes mental pain. It's because of clinging that aging, illness, and death cause mental distress. The paradox here is that, in clinging to things, we don't trap them or get them under our control. Instead, we trap ourselves. When we realize our captivity, we naturally search for a way out. And this is where it's so important that the first noble truth *not* say that "Life is suffering." If life were suffering, where would we look for an end to suffering? We'd be left with nothing but death and annihilation. But when the actual truth is that clinging is suffering, we simply have to look for the clinging and eliminate its causes.

This process takes time, though, because we can't simply tell the mind not to cling. It's like a disobedient child: if you force it to let go while you're looking, it'll search for a blind spot where you can't see it, and will start to cling there. In fact, the mind's major blind spot—ignorance—is the prime cause that gives rise to clinging's proximate cause: craving. So, as the fourth noble truth, the Buddha recommends a path of practice to get rid of the blind spot. The path has eight factors: right view, right resolve, right speech, right action, right livelihood, right effort, right mindfulness, and right concentration. In a more abbreviated form, the Buddha's term for the practice is "abandoning and developing": abandoning activities that get hinder awareness, and developing qualities that expand its clarity and range.

The *abandoning*—in which you refrain from unskillful thoughts, words, and deeds inspired by craving—is obviously an antidote to clinging. The *developing*, though, plays a more paradoxical role, for you have to hold to the skillful qualities of mindfulness, concentration, and discernment that foster awareness until they're fully mature. Only then can you let them go. It's like climbing a ladder to get on a roof: you grab hold of a higher rung so that you can let go of a lower rung, and then grab onto a rung still higher. As the rungs get further off the ground, your view gets more expansive and you can see precisely where the mind's clingings are. You get a sharper sense of which parts of experience belong to which noble truth and what should be done with them: the parts that are suffering should be comprehended; the parts that cause suffering should be abandoned; the parts that form the path to the end of suffering should be further developed; and the parts that belong to the end of suffering should be verified. This helps you get higher and higher on the ladder until you find yourself securely on the roof. That's when you can finally let go of the ladder and be totally free.

So the real question we face is not God's question, passing judgment on how skillfully he created life or the world. It's *our* question: how skillfully are we handling the raw stuff of life? Are we clinging in ways that serve only to continue the round of suffering, or are we learning to hold to the ladder-like qualities that will eliminate craving and ignorance so that we can grow up and not have to cling. If we negotiate life armed with all four noble truths, realizing that life contains both suffering and an end to suffering, there's hope: hope that we'll be able to sort out which parts of life belong to which truth; hope that someday, in this life, we'll discover the brightness at the point where we can agree with the Buddha, "Oh. Yes. This is the end of suffering and stress."

Opening the Door to the Dhamma

Respect in Buddhist Thought & Practice

If you're born into an Asian Buddhist family, the first thing your parents will teach you about Buddhism is not a philosophical tenet but a gesture of respect: how to place your hands in *añjali*, palm-to-palm over your heart, when you encounter a Buddha image, a monk, or a nun. Obviously, the gesture will be mechanical at first. Over time, though, you'll learn the respectful attitude that goes with it. If you're quick to pick it up, your parents will consider it a sign of intelligence, for respect is basic to any ability to learn.

As you get older, they may teach you the symbolism of the gesture: that your hands form a lotus bud, representing your heart, which you are holding out to be trained in how to become wise. Ultimately, as you grow more familiar with the fruits of Buddhist practice, your parents hope that your respect will turn into reverence and veneration. In this way, they give a quick answer to the old Western question of which side of Buddhism—the philosophy or the religion—comes first. In their eyes, the religious attitude of respect is needed for any philosophical understanding to grow. And as far as they're concerned, there's no conflict between the two. In fact, they're mutually reinforcing.

This stands in marked contrast to the typical Western attitude, which sees an essential discrepancy between Buddhism's religious and philosophical sides. The philosophy seems so rational, placing such a high value on self-reliance. The insight at the heart of the Buddha's awakening was so abstract—a principle of causality. There seems no inherent reason for a philosophy with such an abstract beginning to have produced a devotionalism intense enough to rival anything found in the theistic religions.

Yet if we look at what the Pali canon has to say about devotionalism—the attitude it expresses with the cluster of words, *respect, deference, reverence, homage,* and *veneration*—we find not only that its theory of respect is rooted in the central insight of the Buddha's awakening—the causal principle called this/that conditionality *(idappaccayatā)*—but also that respect is required to learn and master this causal principle in the first place.

On the surface it may seem strange to relate a theory of causality to the issue of respect, but the two are intimately entwined. Respect is the attitude you develop toward the things that matter in life. Theories of causality tell you if anything really matters, and if so, *what* matters and *how.* If you believe that a supreme being will grant you happiness, you'll naturally show respect and reverence for that being. If you assume happiness to be entirely self-willed, your greatest respect will be reserved for your own willfulness. As for the *how:* If you view true happiness as totally impossible, totally pre-determined, or totally random, respect is unnecessary, for it makes no difference in the outcome of your life. But if you see true happiness as possible, and its causes as precarious, contingent, and dependent on your attitude, you'll naturally show them the care and respect needed to keep them healthy and strong.

This is reflected in the way the canon treats the issue of respect. It details the varied ways in which lay people of the Buddha's time showed respect to the Buddha and the monastic Saṅgha, and the more standardized ways in which the members of the Saṅgha showed respect to the Buddha and to one another. Especially interesting is the protocol of respect for the Dhamma. Buddhist monks and nuns are forbidden from teaching the Dhamma to anyone who shows disrespect, and the Buddha himself is said to have refused to teach his first sermon to the five brethren until they stopped treating him as a mere equal.

This protocol, of course, may have been a cultural accident, something picked up willy-nilly from the society of the Buddha's time, but there are passages in the canon suggesting otherwise. Buddhism was one of the *samaṇa* (contemplative) movements in ancient India, which claimed to follow truths of nature rather than mainstream cultural norms. These movements were very free in choosing what to adopt from prevailing customs. Buddhist descriptions of other samaṇa movements often criticized them for being disrespectful not only to outsiders but also among themselves. Students are shown being disrespectful to their teachers—their group meetings raucous, noisy, and out of control. All of this is then contrasted with the way Buddhists conduct their meetings in mutual courtesy and respect. This suggests that the Buddhists were free to reject the common customs of respect but made a conscious choice not to.

This choice is based on their insight into respect as a prerequisite for learning. It's easier to learn from someone you respect than from someone you don't. Respect opens the mind and loosens preconceived opinions to make room for new knowledge and skills. At the same time, people who value their knowledge feel more inclined to teach it to someone who shows respect than to someone who doesn't.

However, the type of learning the Buddha emphasizes is not simply the acquisition of information. It's a skill leading to total release from suffering and stress. And this is where the issue of respect connects with causality, for the Buddhist theory of causality centers on the question of how it's possible to learn a skill.

As cybernetics theory shows, learning in general is possible only where there is feedback; learning a skill requires the further ability to monitor feedback and choose how to use it to modify behavior. The Buddha's discoveries in causality explain the *how* and the *what* that allow for these factors. The *how* he expressed as a causal formula; the *what,* as an analysis of action: the factors that shape it, together with the range of results it can give.

The causal formula, simply put, states that each moment is composed of three things: results from past actions, present actions, and the immediate results of present actions. Although this principle seems simple, its consequences are very complex. Every act you perform has repercussions in the present moment that also reverberate into the future. Depending on the intensity of the act, those reverberations can last for a very short or a very long time. Thus every conditioned experience is shaped by the combined effects of past actions coming from a wide range over time, together with the effects of present acts.

Causality over time places certain limitations on each moment. The present is not a clean slate, for it's partially shaped by influences from the past. Immediate causality in the present, however, makes room for free will. Not everything is determined by the past. At any moment, you can insert new input into the process and nudge your life in a new direction. Still, there's not so much room for free will that causality becomes arbitrary.

Every *this* put into the system produces a particular type of *that*. Events follow discernible patterns that can be mastered.

The *what* that keeps this process in motion is the factor allowing for feedback and the monitoring of feedback. The central element in that *what* is intention, which the Buddha identified as the essence of action, or kamma. Intention, in turn, is shaped by acts of attention, which ask questions about perceptions and create views from those questions. Because you can attend to the results of your intentions, there is an internal feedback loop allowing you to learn. Because attention can ask questions, it can monitor that feedback to determine how best to put it to use. And because your intentions—guided by views and offering new input into the present—can then reshape your experience, your ability to learn can make a difference: you can change your behavior and reap the results of your improved skills in terms of greater and greater happiness.

How far can that happiness go? In the course of his Awakening, the Buddha discovered that the pursuit of skillfulness can ultimately lead beyond time and space, beyond the realm of conditionality and rebirth. From this discovery he identified four types of kamma: the first three giving pleasant, painful, or mixed results in the round of rebirth, and the fourth leading beyond all kamma to the end of rebirth. In other words, the principle of causality works so that actions can either continue the round or bring it to an end. Because even the highest pleasure within the round is inconstant and undependable, he taught that the most worthy course of action is the fourth kind of kamma—the type that led to his Awakening—to put an end to kamma once and for all.

The skill needed for this form of kamma comes from coordinating the factors of attention and intention so that they lead first to pleasant results within the round of rebirth, and then— on the transcendent level—to total release from suffering and stress. This, in turn, requires certain attitudes toward the principle of causality operating in human life. And this is where the quality of respect becomes essential, for without the proper respect for three things—yourself, the principle of causality operating in your life, and other people's insights into that principle—you won't be able to muster the resolve needed to master that principle and to see how far your potential for skillfulness can go.

Respect for yourself, in the context of this/that conditionality, means two things:

1) Because the fourth kind of kamma is possible, you can respect your desire for unconditional happiness, and don't have to regard it as an unrealistic ideal.

2) Because of the importance of intention and attention in shaping your experience, you can respect your ability to develop the skills needed to understand and master causal reality to the point of attaining true happiness.

But respect for yourself goes even further than that. Not only *can* you respect your desire for true happiness and your ability to attain it, you *must* respect these things if you don't want to fall under the sway of the many religious and secular forces within society and yourself that would pull you in other directions.

Although most religious cultures assume true happiness to be possible, they don't see human skillfulness as capable of bringing it about. By and large, they place their hopes for happiness in higher powers. As for secular cultures, they don't believe that unconditional happiness is possible at all. They teach us to strive for happiness dependent on conditions, and to turn a blind eye to the limitations inherent in any happiness coming from money, power, relationships, possessions, or a sentimental sense of community. They often scoff at higher values and smile when religious idols fall or religious aspirants show feet of clay.

These secular attitudes foster our own unskillful qualities, our desire to take whatever pleasures come easily, and our impatience with anyone who would tell us that we're capable of better and more. But both the secular and the common religious attitudes teach us to underestimate the powers of our own skillful mind states. Qualities like mindfulness, concentration, and discernment, when they first arise in the mind, seem unremarkable—small and tender, like maple seedlings growing in the midst of weeds. If we don't watch for them or accord them any special respect, the weeds will strangle them or we ourselves will tread them underfoot. As a result, we'll never get to know how much shade they can provide.

If, however, we develop strong respect for our own ability to attain true happiness, two important moral qualities take charge of our minds and watch out for our good qualities: concern for the suffering we'll experience if we don't try our best to develop skillfulness, and shame at the thought of aiming lower than at the highest possible happiness. Shame may seem a strange adjunct to self-respect, but when both are healthy they go together. You need self-respect to recognize when a course of action is beneath you, and that you'd be ashamed to follow it. You need to feel shame for your mistakes in order to keep your self-respect from turning into stubborn pride.

This is where the second aspect of respect—*respect for the principle of causality*—comes in. This/that conditionality is not a free-form process. Each unskillful *this* is connected to an unpleasant *that*. You can't twist the connection to lead to pleasant results, or use your own preferences to design a customized path to release from causal experience. Self-respect thus has to accommodate a respect for the way causes actually produce effects. Traditionally, this respect is expressed in terms of the quality the Buddha stressed in his very last words: heedfulness. To be heedful means having a strong sense that if you're careless in your intentions, you'll suffer. If you truly love yourself, you have to pay close attention to the way reality really works, and act accordingly. Not everything you think or feel is worthy of respect. Even the Buddha himself didn't design Buddhism or the principle of this/that conditionality. He discovered them. Instead of viewing reality in line with his preferences, he reordered his preferences to make the most of what he learned by watching—with scrupulous care and honesty—his actions and their actual effects.

This point is reflected in his discourse to the Kalamas (AN III.66). Although this discourse is often cited as the Buddha's carte blanche for following your own sense of right and wrong, it actually says something very different: *Don't simply follow traditions, but don't simply follow your own preferences, either. If you see, through watching your own actions and their results, that following a certain mental state leads to harm and suffering, you should abandon it and resolve never to follow it again.* This is a rigorous standard, which requires putting the Dhamma ahead of your own preconceived preferences. And it requires that you be very heedful of any tendency to reverse that priority and put your preferences first.

In other words, you can't simply indulge in the pleasure or resist the pain coming from your own actions. You have to learn from both pleasure and pain, to show them respect as events in a causal chain, to see what they have to teach you. This is why the

Buddha called *dukkha*—pain, stress, and suffering—a noble truth; and why he termed the pleasure arising from the concentrated mind a noble truth as well. These aspects of immediate experience contain lessons that can take the mind to the noble attainments.

The discourse to the Kalamas, however, doesn't stop with immediate experience. It goes further and states that, when observing the processes of cause and effect in your actions, you should also confirm your observations with the teachings of the wise. This third aspect of respect—*respect for the insights of others*—is also based on the pattern of this/that conditionality. Because causes are sometimes separated from their effects by great expanses of time, it's easy to lose sight of some important connections. At the same time, your chief obstacle to discernment—delusion—is the mental quality you have the hardest time detecting in yourself. When you're deluded, you don't *know* you're deluded. So the wise approach is to show respect to the insights of others, in the event that their insights may help you see through your own ignorance. After all, intention and attention are immediately present to their awareness as well. Their insights may be just what you need to cut through the obstacles you've created for yourself through your own acts of ignorance.

The Buddhist teachings on respect for other people point in two directions. First, the obvious one: respect for those ahead of you on the path. As the Buddha once said, friendship with admirable people is the whole of the holy life, for their words and examples will help get you on the path to release. This doesn't mean that you need to obey their teachings or accept them unthinkingly. You simply owe it to yourself to give them a respectful hearing and their teachings an honest try. Even—especially—when their advice is unpleasant, you should treat it with respect. As Dhammapada 76 states,

> *Regard him as one who*
> *points out*
> *treasure,*
> *the wise one who*
> *seeing your faults*
> *rebukes you.*
> *Stay with this sort of sage.*
> *For the one who stays*
> *with a sage of this sort,*
> *things get better,*
> *not worse.*

At the same time, when you show respect for those who have mastered the path, you're also showing respect for qualities you want to develop in yourself. And when such people see that you respect the good qualities both in them and in yourself, they'll feel more inclined to share their wisdom with you, and more careful about sharing only their best. This is why the Buddhist tradition places such an emphasis on not only *feeling* respect but also *showing* it. If you can't force yourself to show respect to others in ways they'll recognize, there's a resistance in your mind. They, in turn, will doubt your willingness to learn. This is why the monastic discipline places so much emphasis on the etiquette of respect to be shown to teachers and senior monastics.

The teachings on respect, however, go in another direction as well. Buddhist monks and nuns are not allowed to show disrespect for *anyone* who criticizes them, regardless of whether or not that person is awakened or the criticism well-founded. Critics of this sort may not deserve the level of respect due to teachers, but they do deserve common courtesy. Even unawakened people may have observed valuable bits and pieces of the truth. If you open yourself to criticism, you may get to hear worthwhile insights that a wall of disrespect would have repelled. Buddhist literature—from the earliest days up to the present—abounds with stories of people who gained Awakening after hearing a chance word or song from an unlikely source. A person with the proper attitude of respect can learn from anything—and the ability to put anything to a good use is the mark of true discernment.

Perhaps the most delicate skill with regard to respect is learning how to balance all three aspects of respect: for yourself, for the truth of causality, and for the insight of others. This balance is essential to any skill. If you want to become a potter, for example, you have to learn not only from your teacher, but also from your own actions and powers of observation, and from the clay itself. Then you have to weigh all of these factors together to achieve mastery on your own. If, in your pursuit of the Buddhist path, your self-respect outweighs your respect for the truth of causality or the insights of others, you'll find it hard to take criticism or to laugh at your own foolishness. This will make it impossible for you to learn. If, on the other hand, your respect for your teachers outweighs your self-respect or your respect for the truth, you can open yourself to charlatans and close yourself to the truth that the canon says "is to be seen by the wise for themselves."

The parallels between the role of respect in Buddhist practice and in manual skills explains why many Buddhist teachers require their students to master a manual skill as a prerequisite or a part of their meditation. A person with no manual skills will have little intuitive understanding of how to balance respect. What sets the Buddha's apart from other skills, though, is the level of total freedom it produces. And the difference between that freedom and its alternative—endless rounds of suffering through birth after birth, death after death—is so extreme that we can easily understand why people committed to the pursuit of that freedom show it a level of respect that's also extreme. Even more understandable is the absolute level of respect for that freedom shown by those who have attained it. They bow down to all their inner and outer teachers with the sincerest, most heart-felt gratitude. To see them bow down in this way is an inspiring sight.

So when Buddhist parents teach their children to show respect for the Buddha, Dhamma, and Saṅgha, they aren't teaching them a habit that will later have to be unlearned. Of course, the child will need to discover how best to understand and make use of that respect, but at least the parents have helped open the door for the child to learn from its own powers of observation, to learn from the truth, and to learn from the insights of others. And when that door—when the mind—is opened to what truly deserves respect, all things noble and good can come in.

Questions of Skill

The Buddha wasn't the sort of teacher who simply answered questions. He also taught which questions to ask. He understood the power of questions: that they give shape to the holes in your knowledge and force that shape—valid or not—onto the answers you hope will fill up those holes. Even if you use right information to answer a wrong question, it can take on the wrong shape. If you then use that answer as a tool, you're sure to apply it to the wrong situations and end up with the wrong results.

That's why the Buddha was careful to map out a science of questions, showing which questions—in what order—lead to freedom, and which ones don't. At the same time, he gave his talks in a question-and-answer format, to make perfectly clear the shape of the questions he was answering.

So if you're looking to his teaching for answers and want to get the most out of them, you should first be clear about what questions you're bringing to it, and check to see if they're in line with the questions the teachings were meant to address. That way your answers won't lead you astray.

A case in point is the teaching on not-self. Many students interpret this as the Buddha's answer to two of the most frequently-asked questions in the history of serious thought: "Who am I?" and "Do I have a true self?" In the light of these questions, the teaching seems to be a no-self teaching, saying either an unqualified No: There is no self; or a qualified No: no *separate* self. But the one time the Buddha was asked point-blank if there is a self, he refused to answer, on the grounds that either a Yes or a No to the question would lead to extreme forms of wrong view that block the path to awakening. A Yes or a qualified No would lead to attachment: you'd keep clinging to a sense of self however you defined it. An unqualified No would lead to bewilderment and alienation, for you'd feel that your innermost sense of intrinsic worth had been denied.

As for the question, "Who am I?" the Buddha included it in a list of dead-end questions that lead to "a thicket of views, a wilderness of views, a contortion, a writhing, a fetter of views. Bound by a fetter of views, [you] don't gain freedom from birth, aging, and death, from sorrow, lamentation, pain, distress, or despair." In other words, any attempt to answer either of these questions is unskillful karma, blocking the path to true freedom.

So if the not-self teaching isn't meant to answer these questions, what question *does* it answer? A basic one: "What is skillful?" In fact, *all* of the Buddha's teachings are direct or indirect answers to this question. His great insight was that all our knowledge and ignorance, all our pleasure and pain, come from our actions, our karma, so the quest for true knowledge and true happiness comes down to a question of skill. In this case, the precise question is: "Is self-identification skillful?" And the answer is: "Only up to a point." In the areas where you need a healthy sense of self to act skillfully, it's wise to maintain that sense of self. But eventually, as skillful behavior becomes second nature and you develop more sensitivity, you see that self-identification, even of the most refined sort, is harmful and stressful. You have to let it go.

So, as with any skill, there are definite steps along the road to mastery. And because the asking of a question is a type of karma, the questions you ask not only have to start with the issue of skill, they also have to be skillful—to approach the issue skillfully—themselves. Each step in the Buddha's skill is thus defined by a set of questions that focus your attention and shape your thinking in the most strategic direction. In fact, the questions he recommends can be taken as a map to the practice: you start out with questions that assume a self and use that assumption to motivate yourself to act more and more skillfully. Only when you reach an appropriate level of skill do the questions turn to deconstruct your sense of self, pinpointing the things you identify as your self and showing that they're not really you. When the act of self-identification runs out of options, it stops in mid-air—and the mind opens to freedom. So if you put the not-self teaching in its proper context—this regimen of questions—you'll see that it's not a dead-end answer to a dead-end question. Instead, it's a cutting-edge tool for bringing about liberation.

To begin this regimen, the Buddha recommends that when you visit a teacher, the first questions to ask are these: "What is skillful? What is unskillful? What, if I do it, will be for my long-term harm and suffering? Or what, if I do it, will be for my long-term well-being and happiness?" Although these last two questions bring in the concepts of "I" and "my," they aren't the focus of the inquiry. The focus is on doing, on developing skill, on using your concern for "me" and "my well-being" to train your actions toward true happiness.

The Buddha's answers to these preliminary questions read like a course in wilderness survival. First come the do's and don'ts. A wilderness instructor will tell you: "If a moose charges you, run. If a bear charges you, don't." The Buddha's corresponding do's and don'ts are ten guidelines dealing with body, speech, and mind. The guidelines for the body are: don't kill, don't steal, don't engage in illicit sex. For speech: don't tell lies, don't speak divisively, don't speak abusively, don't engage in idle chatter. And for the mind: abandon greed, abandon ill will, cultivate right views. These are the Buddha's basic ground rules for the survival of your happiness, and many of his teachings simply elaborate on these ten points.

But as any wilderness instructor will tell you, survival requires more than simple rules of thumb. You have to be alert to the gaps not covered by the rules. You need to learn to use your powers of observation, imagination, and ingenuity to dig out unskillful habits and develop new habits to fill in the gaps. That way you can live comfortably in the wilderness, respectful of the bears and moose and other dangers around you without being overwhelmed by them.

The same holds true with the Buddha's skill: in addition to following the do's and don'ts, you have to learn how to dig out the roots of unskillful behavior so that you can become adept in all areas of your life, including the areas where the do's and don'ts don't apply. The roots of unskillful behavior are three: greed, anger, and delusion. Of the three, delusion is the most insidious, for it blinds you to its very existence. The only way to overcome it is to be relentlessly observant, looking at your actions in terms of cause and effect, gauging their short- and long-term consequences for yourself and others.

Again, this involves learning to ask the right questions. Each time you're about to act, ask yourself: "This action that I want to do: would it lead to self-harm, to the harm of others, or to both? Is it an unskillful action, with painful consequences, painful results?" If you foresee harm, don't follow through with it. If not,

go ahead and act. While acting, ask yourself if there are any unexpected bad consequences arising. If there are, stop. If there aren't,
continue with what you're doing. When the action is done, look
into its actual short- and long-term consequences. If an action in
word or deed has ended up causing harm, inform an experienced
fellow-practitioner on the path (this is why the Buddha established the Saṅgha) and listen to that person's advice. If the
mistaken action was purely an act of the mind, try to develop distaste for that kind of thinking. In both cases, resolve never to
make the same mistake again, and use your ingenuity to make
the resolve stick. If, however, the long-term consequences of the
original action were harmless, take joy and satisfaction in being
on the right path and continue your training.

As you stay with this line of questioning, it fosters two
major results. To begin with, you become more sensitive to your
actions and respectful of their effects, both in the present and
over time. Unlike the child who says, "It was already broken
when I stepped on it," you're aware of when you break things—
physical or mental—and when you don't. At the same time, you
gain mastery over the patterns of action and effect. You get
better and better at handling things without their getting
broken. This in turn fosters a healthy sense of "self" and "I"
based on competence and skill. Your sense of self becomes
good-humored enough to freely admit mistakes, mature enough
to learn from them, quick enough to notice the immediate
effects of your actions, while patient enough to strive for long-
term goals. Confident in its own powers of observation, this "I"
also has the humility needed to learn from the experience and
advice of others.

These two results—sensitivity to the effects of your own
actions and a competent sense of self—enable you to settle into a
level of mental concentration that's solid and nourishing. You
overcome the hindrance of uncertainty as to what's skillful and
unskillful, and are able to develop the skillful qualities needed to
center the mind. As this centered focus develops, an interesting
thing happens: your sensitivity to actions and your sense of self
come face to face. You begin to see that self not as a thing but as
an activity, a process of "I-making" and "my-making" in which
you repeatedly create and re-create your sense of who you are.
You also begin to notice that this I-making, even when it produces the most skillful self possible, inevitably results in stress.

Why? Because any sense of "I" or "mine" involves clinging—even when your concentration tunes into a sense of
universal self—and all clinging is stressful. So to take the development of skillfulness to its ultimate degree, you have to
unlearn the habit of I-making and my-making. And to do this,
another set of questions is required.

These are the questions that introduce the strategy of not-
self. The Buddha recommends that you focus on any
phenomenon around which you might sense an "I" or a "mine,"
and ask a series of questions, starting with: "Is this constant or
inconstant?" If you identify with your body, look at it. You'll see
that it grows hungry and thirsty, that it's aging, destined to
grow ill and die. "And is anything inconstant easeful or stressful?" Look at any attempt to find a stable happiness based on
the body, and you'll see how stressful it is. "And is it fitting to
regard what's inconstant, stressful, subject to change as: 'This is
mine. This is my self. This is what I am'?"

Pursue this line of inquiry inward, through layer after layer
of physical and mental events, until you can zero in on the high
command: the self that's managing not only the stability of your
concentration but also your internal dialogue of questions and
answers. Fortified with the sense of stability and calm that come
with strong concentration, you can start deconstructing that self
with no anxiety over what will happen when it's gone. And
when the intentions making up that self are deconstructed, a
strange thing happens. It's as if you had pulled out a strategic
thread holding a tapestry together, and now the whole thing
unravels on its own. Everything that could possibly be clung to
falls away. What remains is total, absolute freedom—free from
time and space, from both self and not-self, for both "self" and
"not-self" are perceptions, which that freedom transcends.

Even when you've had only a first, humbling taste of this
freedom, you appreciate how adroitly the teaching on not-self
answers the question of "What is skillful?" And you understand
why the Buddha recommends putting the question of "Who am
I?" aside. To begin with, it wouldn't have taken you to this freedom, and could well have stood in freedom's way. Because your
"I" is an activity, any attempt to pin it down before you had
mastered the processes of activity would have left you pouncing
on shadows, distracted from the real work at hand. Any attempt
to deconstruct your "I" before it had become healthy and

mature would have led to a release neurotic and insecure: you'd simply be running away from the messy, mismanaged parts of your life. In addition, any answer to the question "Who am I?" would be totally inappropriate to describe your new-found freedom, for it's a dimension apart, where the concepts of "I," "not-I," "am," "am not" do not apply.

The only question still concerning you is how to dig out the remaining roots of unskillfulness still latent in the mind. Once they're dug up, the Buddha promises, nothing stands in the way to full and final freedom. And in that freedom, the mind lacks nothing, has nothing in excess. There's none of the delusion that would shape the hole of a burning question, and none of the greed or aversion that would give it teeth. The only remaining questions are bonus ones: how best to take whatever skills you've developed along the way and use them purely for the benefit of the world.

And what more could you possibly ask?

Freedom from Fear

An anthropologist once questioned an Alaskan shaman about his tribe's belief system. After putting up with the anthropologist's questions for a while, the shaman finally told him: "Look. We don't believe. We fear."

His words have intrigued me ever since I first heard them. I've also been intrigued by the responses I get when I share his words with my friends. Some say that the shaman unconsciously put his finger on the line separating primitive religion from civilized religion: primitive religion is founded on childish fear; civilized religion, on love, trust, and joy. Others maintain that the shaman cut through the pretensions and denials of civilized religion and pointed to the true source of all serious religious life.

If we dig down to the assumptions underlying these two responses, we find that the first response views fear itself as our greatest weakness. If we can simply overcome fear, we put ourselves in a position of strength. The second sees fear as the most honest response to our greater weakness in the face of aging, illness, and death—a weakness that can't be overcome with a simple shift in attitude. If we're not in touch with our honest fears, we won't feel motivated to do what's needed to protect ourselves from genuine dangers.

So—which attitude toward fear is childish, and which is mature? Is there an element of truth in both? If so, how can those elements best be combined? These questions are best answered by rephrasing them: To what extent is fear a useful emotion? To what extent is it not? Does it have a role in the practice that puts an end to fear?

The Buddhist answer to these questions is complex. This is due partly to Buddhism's dual roots—both as a civilized and as a wilderness tradition—and also to the complexity of fear itself, even in its most primal forms. Think of a deer at night suddenly caught in a hunter's headlights. It's confused. Angry. It senses danger, and that it's weak in the face of the danger. It wants to escape. These five elements—confusion, aversion, a sense of danger, a sense of weakness, and a desire to escape—are present, to a greater or lesser extent, in every fear. The confusion and aversion are the unskillful elements. Even if the deer has many openings to escape from the hunter, its confusion and aversion might cause it to miss them. The same holds true for human beings. The mistakes and evils we commit when finding ourselves weak in the face of danger come from confusion and aversion.

Maddeningly, however, there are also evils that we commit out of complacency, when oblivious to actual dangers: the callous things we do when we feel we can get away with them. Thus the last three elements of fear—the perception of weakness, the perception of danger, and the desire to escape it—are needed to avoid the evils coming from complacency. If stripped of confusion and aversion, these three elements become a positive quality, heedfulness—something so essential to the practice that the Buddha devoted his last words to it. The dangers of life are real. Our weaknesses are real. If we don't see them clearly, don't take them to heart, and don't try to find a way out, there's no way we can put an end to what causes our fears. Just like the deer: if it's complacent about the hunter's headlights, it's going to end up strapped to the fender for sure.

So to genuinely free the mind from fear, we can't simply deny that there's any reason for fear. We have to overcome the basic cause of fear: the mind's weaknesses in the face of very real dangers. The elegance of the Buddha's approach to this problem, though, lies in his insight into the confusion—or to use the standard Buddhist term, delusion—that makes fear unskillful. Despite the complexity of fear, delusion is the single factor that, in itself, is both the mind's prime weakness and its greatest danger. Thus the Buddha approaches the problem of fear by focusing on delusion, and he attacks delusion in two ways: getting us to *think about* its dangerous role in making fear unskillful, and to *develop* inner strengths leading to the insights that cut through the delusions that make the mind weak. In this way we not only overcome the factor that makes fear unskillful. We ultimately put the mind in a position where it has no need for fear.

When we think about how delusion infects fear and incites us to do unskillful things, we see that it can act in two ways. First, the delusions surrounding our fears can cause us to misapprehend the dangers we face, seeing danger where there is none, and no danger where there is. If we obsess over non-existent or trivial dangers, we'll squander time and energy building up useless defenses, diverting our attention from genuine threats. If, on the other hand, we put the genuine dangers of aging, illness, and death out of our minds, we grow complacent in our actions. We let ourselves cling to things—our bodies, our loved ones, our possessions, our views—that leave us exposed to aging, illness, separation, and death in the first place. We allow our cravings to take charge of the mind, sometimes to the point of doing evil with impunity, thinking we're immune to the results of our evil, that those results will never return to harm us.

The more complacent we are about the genuine dangers lying in wait all around us, the more shocked and confused we become when they actually hit. This leads to the second way in which the delusions surrounding our fears promote unskillful actions: we react to genuine dangers in ways that, instead of ending the dangers, actually create new ones. We amass wealth to provide security, but wealth creates a high profile that excites jealousy in others. We build walls to keep out dangerous people, but those walls become our prisons. We stockpile weapons, but they can easily be turned against us.

The most unskillful response to fear is when, perceiving dangers to our own life or property, we believe that we can gain strength and security by destroying the lives and property of others. The delusion pervading our fear makes us lose perspective. If other people were to act in this way, we would know they were wrong. But somehow, when we feel threatened, our standards change, our perspective warps, so that wrong seems right as long as *we're* the ones doing it.

This is probably the most disconcerting human weakness of all: our inability to trust ourselves to do the right thing when the chips are down. If standards of right and wrong are meaningful only when we find them convenient, they have no real meaning at all.

Fortunately, though, the area of life posing the most danger and insecurity is the area where, through training, we can make the most changes and exercise the most control. Although aging, illness, and death follow inevitably on birth, delusion doesn't. It can be prevented. If, through thought and contemplation, we become heedful of the dangers it poses, we can feel motivated to overcome it. However, the insights coming from

simple thought and contemplation aren't enough to fully understand and overthrow delusion. It's the same as with any
revolution: no matter how much you may think about the
matter, you don't really know the tricks and strengths of
entrenched powers until you amass your own troops and do
battle with them. And only when your own troops develop
their own tricks and strengths can they come out on top. So it is
with delusion: only when you develop mental strengths can you
see through the delusions that give fear its power. Beyond that,
these strengths can put you in a position where you are no
longer exposed to dangers ever again.

The canon lists these mental strengths at five: conviction,
persistence, mindfulness, concentration, and discernment. It
also emphasizes the role that heedfulness plays in developing
each, for heedfulness is what enables each strength to counteract a particular delusion that makes the mind weak and
unskillful in the face of its fears. What this means is that none of
these strengths are mere brute forces. Each contains an element
of wisdom and discernment, which gets more penetrating as
you progress along the list.

Of the five strengths, conviction requires the longest explanation, both because it's one of the most misunderstood and
under-appreciated factors in the Buddhist path, and because of
the multiple delusions it has to counteract.

The conviction here is conviction in the principle of karma:
that the pleasure and pain we experience depends on the quality of the intentions on which we act. This conviction
counteracts the delusion that "It's not in my best interest to stick
to moral principles in the face of danger," and it attacks this
delusion in three ways.

First, it insists on what might be called the "boomerang" or
"spitting into the wind" principle of karmic cause and effect. If
you act on harmful intentions, regardless of the situation, the
harm will come back to you. Even if unskillful actions such as
killing, stealing, or lying might bring short-term advantages,
these are more than offset by the long-term harm to which they
leave you exposed.

Conversely, this same principle can make you brave in doing
good. If you're convinced that the results of skillful intentions
will have to return to you even if death intervenes, you can more
easily make the sacrifices demanded by long-term endeavors for

your own good and that of others. Whether of not you live to see the results in this lifetime, you're convinced that the good you do is never lost. In this way, you develop the courage needed to build a store of skillful actions—generous and virtuous—that forms your first line of defense against dangers and fear.

Second, conviction insists on giving priority to your state of mind above all else, for that's what shapes your intentions. This counteracts the corollary to the first delusion: "What if sticking to my principles makes it easier for people to do me harm?" This question is based ultimately on the delusion that life is our most precious possession. If that were true, it would be a pretty miserable possession, for it heads inexorably to death, with holdovers in pain, aging, and illness along the way. Conviction views our life as precious only to the extent that it's used to develop the mind, for the mind—when developed—is something that no one, not even death, can harm. "Quality of life" is measured by the quality and integrity of the intentions on which we act, just as "quality time" is time devoted to the practice. Or, in the Buddha's words:

> *Better than a hundred years*
> *lived without virtue, uncentered, is*
> > *one day*
> *lived by a virtuous person*
> *absorbed in jhāna. (Dhp 110)*

Third, conviction insists that the need for integrity is unconditional. Even though other people may throw away their most valuable possession—their integrity—it's no excuse for us to throw away ours. The principle of karma isn't a traffic ordinance in effect only on certain hours of the day or certain days of the week. It's a law operating around the clock, around the cycles of the cosmos.

Some people have argued that, because the Buddha recognized the principle of conditionality, he would have no problem with the idea that our virtues should depend on conditions as well. This is a misunderstanding of the principle. To begin with, conditionality doesn't simply mean that everything is changeable and contingent. It's like the theory of relativity. Relativity doesn't mean that all things are relative. It simply replaces mass and time—which long were considered constants—with another, unexpected constant: the speed of light. Mass and time may be relative to a particular inertial frame, as the frame relates to the speed of light, but the laws of physics are constant for all inertial frames, regardless of speed. The speed of light is always the same.

In the same way, conditionality means that there are certain unchanging patterns to contingency and change—one of those patterns being that unskillful intentions, based on craving and delusion, invariably lead to unpleasant results.

If we learn to accept this pattern, rather than our feelings and opinions, as absolute, it requires us to become more ingenious in dealing with danger. Instead of following our unskillful knee-jerk reactions, we learn to think outside the box to find responses that best prevent harm of any kind. This gives our actions added precision and grace.

At the same time, we have to note that the Buddha didn't teach conditionality simply to encourage acceptance for the inevitability of change. He taught it to show how the patterns underlying change can be mastered to create an opening that leads beyond conditionality and change. If we want to reach the unconditioned—the truest security—our integrity has to be unconditional, a gift of temporal security not only to those who treat us well, but to everyone, without exception. As the texts say, when you abstain absolutely from doing harm, you give a great gift—freedom from danger to limitless beings—and you yourself find a share in that limitless freedom as well.

Conviction and integrity of this sort make great demands on us. Until we gain our first taste of the unconditioned, they can easily be shaken. This is why they have to be augmented with other mental strengths. The three middle strengths—persistence, mindfulness, and concentration—act in concert. Persistence, in the form of right effort, counteracts the delusion that we're no match for our fears, that once they arise we have to give into them. Right effort gives us practice in eliminating milder unskillful qualities and developing skillful ones in their place, so that when stronger unskillful qualities arise, we can use our skillful qualities as allies in fending them off. The strength of mindfulness assists this process in two ways. (1) It reminds us of the danger of giving into fear. (2) It teaches us to focus our attention, not on the object of our fear, but on the fear in and of itself as a mental event, something we can watch from the outside rather jumping in and going along for a ride. The strength of concentration, in providing the mind with a still center of wellbeing, puts us in a solid position where we don't feel compelled to identify with fears as they come, and where the comings and goings of internal and external dangers are less and less threatening to the mind.

Even then, though, the mind can't reach ultimate security until it uproots the causes of these comings and goings, which is why the first four strengths require the strength of discernment to make them fully secure. Discernment is what sees that these comings and goings are ultimately rooted in our sense of "I" and "mine," and that "I" and "mine" are not built into experience. They come from the repeated processes of I-making and my-making, in which we impose these notions on experience and identify with things subject to aging, illness, and death. Furthermore, discernment sees through our inner traitors and weaknesses: the cravings that want us to make an "I" and "mine"; the delusions that make us believe in them once they're made. It realizes that this level of delusion is precisely the factor that makes aging, illness, and death dangerous to begin with. If we didn't identify with things that age, grow ill, and die, their aging, illness, and death wouldn't threaten the mind. Totally unthreatened, the mind would have no reason to do anything unskillful ever again.

When this level of discernment matures and bears the fruit of release, our greatest insecurity—our inability to trust ourselves—has been eliminated. Freed from the attachments of "I" and "mine," we find that the component factors of fear—both skillful and unskillful—are gone. There's no remaining confusion or aversion; the mind is no longer weak in the face of danger; and so there's nothing from which we need to escape.

This is where the questions raised by the shaman's remarks find their answers. We fear because we believe in "we." We believe in "we" because of the delusion in our fear. Paradoxically, though, if we love ourselves enough to fear the suffering that comes from unskillful actions and attachments, and learn to believe in the way out, we'll develop the strengths that allow us to cut through our cravings, delusions, and attachments. That way, the entire complex—the "we," the fear, the beliefs, the attachments—dissolves away. The freedom remaining is the only true security there is.

This teaching may offer cold comfort to anyone who wants the impossible: security for his or her attachments. But in trading away the hope for an impossible security, you gain the reality of a happiness totally independent and condition-free. Once you've made this trade, you know that the pay-off is more than worth the price. As one of the Buddha's students once reported, "Before, when I has a householder, maintaining the bliss of kingship, I had guards posted within and without the royal apartments, within and without the city, within and without the countryside. But even though I was thus guarded, thus protected, I dwelled in fear—agitated, distrustful, and afraid. But now, on going alone to a forest, to the foot of a tree, or to an empty dwelling, I dwell without fear, unagitated, confident, and unafraid—unconcerned, unruffled, my wants satisfied, with my mind like a wild deer. This is the meaning I have in mind that I repeatedly exclaim, 'What bliss! What bliss!'"

His deer is obviously not the deer in the headlights. It's a deer safe in the wilderness, at its ease wherever it goes. What makes it more than a deer is that, free from attachment, it's called a "consciousness without surface." Light goes right through it. The hunter can't shoot it, for it can't be seen.

Samsara

saṁsara literally means "wandering-on." Many people think of it as the Buddhist name for the place where we currently live—the place we leave when we go to nibbana. But in the early Buddhist texts, it's the answer, not to the question , "Where are we?" but to the question, "What are we doing?" Instead of a place, it's a process: the tendency to keep creating worlds and then moving into them. As one world falls apart, you create another one and go there. At the same time, you bump into other people who are creating their own worlds, too.

The play and creativity in the process can sometimes be enjoyable. In fact, it would be perfectly innocuous if it didn't entail so much suffering. The worlds we create keep caving in and killing us. Moving into a new world requires effort: not only the pains and risks of taking birth, but also the hard knocks—mental and physical—that come from going through childhood into adulthood, over and over again. The Buddha once asked his monks, "Which do you think is greater: the water in the oceans or the tears you've shed while wandering on?" His answer: the tears. Think of that the next time you gaze at the ocean or play in its waves.

In addition to creating suffering for ourselves, the worlds we create feed off the worlds of others, just as theirs feed off ours. In some cases the feeding may be mutually enjoyable and beneficial, but even then the arrangement has to come to an end. More typically, it causes harm to at least one side of the relationship, often to both. When you think of all the suffering that goes into keeping just one person clothed, fed, sheltered, and healthy—the suffering both for those who have to pay for these requisites, as well as those who have to labor or die in their production—you see how exploitative even the most rudimentary process of world-building can be.

This is why the Buddha tried to find the way to stop samsara-ing. Once he had found it, he encouraged others to follow it, too. Because samsara-ing is something that each of us does, each of us has to stop it him or her self alone. If samsara were a place, it might seem selfish for one person to look for an escape, leaving others behind. But when you realize that it's a process, there's nothing selfish about stopping it at all. It's like giving up an addiction or an abusive habit. When you learn the skills needed to stop creating your own worlds of suffering, you can share those skills with others so that they can stop creating theirs. At the same time, you'll never have to feed off the worlds of others, so to that extent you're lightening their load as well.

It's true that the Buddha likened the practice for stopping samsara to the act of going from one place to another: from this side of a river to the further shore. But the passages where he makes this comparison often end with a paradox: the further shore has no "here," no "there," no "in between." From that perspective, it's obvious that samsara's parameters of space and time were not the pre-existing context in which we wandered. They were the result of our wandering.

For someone addicted to world-building, the lack of familiar parameters may sound unsettling. But if you're tired of creating incessant, unnecessary suffering, you might want to give it a try. After all, you could always resume building if the lack of "here" or "there" turned out to be dull. But of those who have learned how to break the habit, no one has ever felt tempted to samsara again.

Samsara Divided by Zero

The goal of Buddhist practice, nibbana, is said to be totally uncaused, and right there is a paradox. If the goal is uncaused, how can a path of practice—which is causal by nature—bring it about? This is an ancient question. The *Milinda-pañhā*, a set of dialogues composed near the start of the common era, reports an exchange where King Milinda challenges a monk, Nagasena, with precisely this question. Nagasena replies with an analogy. The path of practice doesn't cause nibbana, he says. It simply takes you there, just as a road to a mountain doesn't cause the mountain to come into being, but simply leads you to where it is.

Nagasena's reply, though apt, didn't really settle the issue within the Buddhist tradition. Over the years many schools of meditation have taught that mental fabrications simply get in the way of a goal that's uncaused and unfabricated. Only by doing nothing at all and thus not fabricating anything in the mind, they say, will the unfabricated shine forth.

This view is based on a very simplistic understanding of fabricated reality, seeing causality as linear and totally predictable: X causes Y which causes Z and so on, with no effects turning around to condition their causes, and no possible way of using causality to escape from the causal network. However, one of the many things the Buddha discovered in the course of his awakening was that causality is not linear. The experience of the present is shaped both by actions in the present and by actions in the past. Actions in the present shape both the present and the future. The results of past and present actions continually interact. Thus there is always room for new input into the system, which gives scope for free will. There is also room for the many feedback loops that make experience so thoroughly complex, and that are so intriguingly described in chaos theory. Reality doesn't resemble a simple line or circle. It's more like the bizarre trajectories of a strange attractor or a Mandelbrot set.

Because there are many similarities between chaos theory and Buddhist explanations of causality, it seems legitimate to explore those similarities to see what light chaos theory can throw on the issue of how a causal path of practice can lead to an uncaused goal. This is not to equate Buddhism with chaos theory, or to engage in pseudo-science. It's simply a search for similes to clear up an apparent conflict in the Buddha's teaching.

And it so happens that one of the discoveries of non-linear math—the basis for chaos theory—throws light on just this issue. In the 19th century, the French mathematician Jules-Henri Poincaré discovered that in any complex physical system there are points he called resonances. If the forces governing the system are described as mathematical equations, the resonances are the points where the equations intersect in such a way that one of the members is divided by zero. This, of course, produces an undefined result, which means that if an object within the system strayed into a resonance point, it would no longer be defined by the causal network determining the system. It would be set free.

In actual practice, it's very rare for an object to hit a resonance point. The equations describing the points immediately around a resonance tend to deflect any incoming object from entering the resonance unless the object is on a precise path to the resonance's very heart. Still, it doesn't take too much complexity to create resonances—Poincaré discovered them while calculating the gravitational interactions among three bodies: the earth, the sun, and the moon. The more complex the system, the greater the number of resonances, and the greater the likelihood that objects will stray into them. It's no wonder that meteors, on a large scale, and electrons on a small scale, occasionally wander right into a resonance in a gravitational or electronic field, and thus to the freedom of total unpredictability. This is why meteors sometimes leave the solar system, and why your computer occasionally freezes for no apparent reason. It's also why strange things could happen someday to the beating of your heart.

If we were to apply this analogy to the Buddhist path, the system we're in is saṁsāra, the round of rebirth. Its resonances would be what the texts called "non-fashioning," the opening to the uncaused: nibbāna. The wall of resistant forces around the resonances would correspond to pain, stress, and attachment. To allow yourself to be repelled by stress or deflected by attachment, no matter how subtle, would be like approaching a resonance but then veering off to another part of the system. But to focus directly on analyzing stress and attachment, and deconstructing their causes, would be like getting on an undeflected trajectory right into the resonance and finding total, undefined freedom.

This, of course, is simply an analogy. But it's a fruitful one for showing that there is nothing illogical in actively mastering the processes of mental fabrication and causality for the sake of going beyond fabrication, beyond cause and effect. At the same time, it gives a hint as to why a path of total inaction would not lead to the unfabricated. If you simply sit still within the system of causality, you'll never get near the resonances where true non-fashioning lies. You'll keep floating around in saṁsāra. But if you take aim at stress and clinging, and work to take them apart, you'll be able to break through to the point where the present moment gets divided by zero in the mind.

The Agendas of Mindfulness

The Pali term for meditation is *bhāvanā:* development. It's a shorthand word for the development of skillful qualities in the mind. Bhavana is a type of karma—the intentional activity leading ultimately leading to the end of karma—but karma nonetheless. This point is underlined by another Pali term for meditation: *kammaṭṭhāna,* the work at hand; and by a Thai idiom for meditation: "to make an effort." These terms are worth keeping in mind, to counterbalance the common assumption that meditation is an exercise in inaction or in passive, all-encompassing acceptance. Actually, as described in the Pali texts, meditation is a very pro-active process. It has an agenda and works actively to bring it about. This can be seen in the Pali description of how of right mindfulness is fostered through *satipaṭṭhāna.*

Satipaṭṭhāna is often translated as "foundation of mindfulness," which gives the impression that it refers to an object of meditation. This impression is reinforced when you see the four satipaṭṭhanas listed as body, feelings, mind, and mental qualities. But if you look at the texts, you find that they teach satipaṭṭhāna as a process, a way of establishing *(upaṭṭhāna)* mindfulness *(sati):* hence the compound term. When the texts define the compound, they give, not a list of objects, but four formulas describing an activity.

Here's the first formula:

> A meditator remains focused on the body in and
> of itself—ardent, alert, and mindful—putting
> aside greed and distress with reference to the
> world.

Each of the terms in this formula is important. "Remaining focused" can also be translated as "keeping track." This refers to the element of concentration in the practice, as you hold to one particular theme or frame of reference amid the conflicting currents of experience. "Ardent" refers to the effort you put into the practice, trying to abandon unskillful states of mind and develop skillful ones in their stead, all the while trying to discern the difference between the two. "Alert" means being clearly aware of what's happening in the present. "Mindful" means being able to remember or recollect. Sometimes mindfulness is translated as non-reactive awareness, free from agendas, simply present with whatever arises, but the formula for satipaṭṭhana doesn't support that translation. Non-reactive awareness is actually part of equanimity, one of many qualities fostered in the course of satipaṭṭhana, but the ardency involved in satipaṭṭhana definitely has an agenda, a task to be done, while the role of mindfulness is to keep your task in mind.

The task here is twofold: staying focused on your frame of reference, and putting aside any greed and distress that would result from shifting your frame of reference back to the world. This is the meaning of "the body in and of itself." In other words, you try to stay with the experience of the body as it's immediately felt, without referring it to the narratives and views that make up your sense of the world. You stay away from stories of how you have related to your body in the past and how you hope to relate to it in the future. You drop any concern for how your body fits into the world in terms of its beauty, agility, or strength. You simply tune into the body on its own terms— the direct experience of its breathing, its movements, its postures, its elementary properties, and its inevitable decay. In this way you learn how to strip away your assumptions about what does or doesn't lie behind your experience of the body, and gain practice in referring everything to the experience itself.

The same approach applies to the remaining types of satipaṭṭhana: focusing on feelings, on mind states, and on mental qualities in and of themselves. At first glance, these may look like new and different meditation exercises, but the Buddha makes clear that they can all center on a single practice: keeping the breath in mind. When the mind is with the breath, all four frames of reference are right there. The difference lies simply in the subtlety of your focus. So when you've developed your skills with the first, most blatant type of satipaṭṭhana, you don't have to move far to take up the more subtle ones. Simply stay with the breath and shift your focus to the feelings and mind states that arise from being mindful of the breath, and the mental qualities that either get in the way of your focus or strengthen it. Once you've chosen your frame of reference, you treat it the same way you've been treating the body: taking it as your frame of reference in and of itself, without referring it to stories about yourself or views about the world. You separate feelings—of pleasure, pain, and neither-pleasure-nor-pain— from the stories you normally create around them. You separate states of greed, anger, and delusion from their focal points in the world. In this way you can see them for what they are.

Still, though, you have an agenda, based on the desire for Awakening—a desire that the Buddha classed, not as a cause of suffering, but as part of the path leading to its end. This becomes clearest in the satipaṭṭhana focused on mental qualities in and of themselves. You acquaint yourself with the unskillful qualities that obstruct concentration—such as sensual desire, ill will, and restlessness—not simply to experience them, but also to understand them so that you can cut them away. Similarly, you acquaint yourself with the skillful qualities that foster discernment so that you can develop them all the way to release.

The texts call these skillful qualities the seven factors of Awakening and show that satipaṭṭhana practice is aimed at developing them all in order. The first factor is mindfulness. The second is called "analysis of qualities": the ability to distinguish skillful from unskillful qualities in the mind, seeing what can be accepted and what needs to be changed. The third factor is persistence—persistence in abandoning unskillful qualities and fostering skillful ones in their place. The texts describe a wide variety of methods to use in this endeavor, but they all come down to two sorts. In some cases, an unskillful quality will disappear simply when you watch it steadily. In other cases, you have to make a concerted effort, actively doing what you can to counteract an unskillful quality and replace it with a more skillful one.

As skillful qualities take charge within you, you see that while skillful thinking leads to no harmful actions, long bouts of it can tire the mind. So you bring your thoughts to stillness, which develops three more of the factors of Awakening: rapture, serenity, and concentration. These provide the mind with a foundation of well-being.

The final factor is equanimity, and its place in the list is significant. Its non-reactivity is fully appropriate only when the more active factors have done what they can. This is true of all the lists in which equanimity is included. It's never listed on its own, as sufficient for Awakening; and it always comes last, after the proactive factors in the list. This doesn't mean that it supplants them, simply that joins in their interaction. Instead of replacing them, it counterbalances them, enabling you to step back and see subtle levels of stress and craving that the more pro-active factors may have obscured. Then it makes room for the pro-active factors to act on the newly discovered levels. Only when all levels of stress and craving are gone is the work of both the pro-active and non-reactive sides of meditation done. That's when the mind can be truly agenda-free.

It's like learning to play the piano. As you get more pro-active in playing proficiently, you also become sensitive in listening non-reactively, to discern ever more subtle levels in the music. This allows you to play even more skillfully. In the same way, as you get more skilled in establishing mindfulness on your chosen frame of reference, you gain greater sensitivity in peeling away ever more subtle layers of the present moment until nothing is left standing in the way of total release.

De-perception

Meditation teaches you the power of your perceptions. You come to see how the labels you apply to things, the images with which you visualize things, have a huge influence over what you see, how they can weigh you down with suffering and stress. As the meditation develops, though, it gives you the tools you need to gain freedom from that influence.

In the beginning, when you first notice the power of perception, you can easily feel overwhelmed by how pervasive it is. Suppose you're focusing on the breath. There comes a point when you begin to wonder whether you're focusing on the breath itself or on your *idea* of the breath. Once this question arises, the normal reaction is to try to get around the idea to the raw sensation behind it. But if you're really sensitive as you do this, you'll notice that you're simply replacing one caricature of the breath with another, more subtle one. Even the raw sensation of breathing is shaped by how you conceptualize raw sensation. No matter how hard you try to pin down an unfiltered experience of breathing, you still find it shaped by your idea of what breathing actually is. The more you pursue the reality of the breath, the more it recedes like a mirage.

The trick here is to turn this fact to your advantage. After all, you're not meditating to get to the breath. You're meditating to understand the processes leading to suffering to that you can put an end to them. The way your relate to your perceptions is part of these processes, so *that's* what you want to see. You have to treat your experience of the breath, not as an end in itself, but as a tool for understanding the role of perception in creating suffering and stress.

You do this by de-perception: questioning your assumptions about breathing, deliberately changing those assumptions, and observing what happens as a result. Now, without the proper context, de-perception could easily wander off into random abstractions. So you take the practice of concentration as your context, providing de-perception both with a general direction and with particular tasks that force it to bump up against the operative assumptions that actually shape your experience of the present.

The general direction lies in trying to bring the mind to deeper and more long-lasting levels of stillness so as to eliminate more and more subtle levels of stress. You're not trying to prove which perceptions of the breath depict it most truly, but simply which ones work best in which situations for eliminating stress. The objectivity you're looking for is not the objectivity of the breath, but the objectivity of cause and effect.

The particular tasks that teach you these lessons begin with the task of trying to get the mind to stay comfortably focused for long periods of time on the breath—and right there you run into two operative assumptions: What does it mean to breathe? What does it mean to be focused?

It's common to think of the breath as the air passing in and out through the nose, and this can be a useful perception to start with. Use whatever blatant sensations you associate with that perception as a means of establishing mindfulness, developing alertness, and getting the mind to grow still. But as your attention gets more refined, you may find that level of breath becoming too faint to detect. So try thinking of the breath instead as the energy flow in the body, as a full body process.

Then make that experience as comfortable as possible. If you feel any blockage or obstruction in the breathing, see what you can do to dissolve those feelings. Are you doing anything to create them? If you can catch yourself creating them, then it's easy to let them dissolve. And what would make you create them aside from your preconceived notions of how the mechanics of breathing have to work? So question those notions: Where does the breath come into the body? Does it come in only through the nose and mouth? Does the body have to pull the breath in? If so, which sensations do the pulling? Which sensations get pulled? Where does the pulling begin? And where is the breath pulled from? Which parts have the breath, and which ones don't? When you feel a sensation of blockage, which side of the sensation are you on?

These questions may sound strange, but many times your pre-verbal assumptions about the body are strange as well. Only when you confront them head-on with strange questions can you bring them to light. And only when you see them clearly can you replace them with alternative concepts.

So once you catch yourself breathing uncomfortably in line with a particular assumption, turn it around to see what sensations the new assumption highlights. Try staying with those sensations as long as you can, to test them. If, compared to your earlier sensations associated with the breath, they're easier to stay with, if they provide a more solid and spacious grounding for concentration, the assumption that drew them to your attention is a useful new tool in your meditation. If the new sensations aren't helpful in that way, you can throw the new tool aside.

For example, if you have a sense of being on one side of a blockage, try thinking of being on the other side. Try being on both. Think of the breath as coming into the body, not through the nose or mouth, but through the middle of the chest, the back of the neck, every pore of your skin, any spot that helps reduce the felt need to push and pull.

Or start questioning the need to push and pull at all. Do you feel that your immediate experience of the body is of the solid parts, and that they have to manage the mechanics of breathing, which is secondary? What happens if you conceive your immediate experience of the body in a different way, as a field of primary breath energy, with the solidity simply a label attached to certain aspects of the breath? Whatever you experience as a primary body sensation, think of it as already breath, without your having to do anything more to it. How does that affect the level of stress and strain in the breathing?

And what about the act of staying focused? How do you conceive that? Is it behind the breath? Surrounded by breath? To what extent does your mental picture of focusing help or hinder the ease and solidity of your concentration? For instance, you may find that you think of the mind as being in one part of the body and not in others. What do you do when you focus attention on another part? Does the mind leave its home base—say, in the head—to go there, or does the other part have to be brought into the head? What kind of tension does this create? What happens if you think of awareness already being in that other part? What happens when you turn things around entirely: instead of the mind's being in the body, see what stress is eliminated when you think of the body as surrounded by a pre-existing field of awareness.

When you ask questions like this and gain favorable results, the mind can settle down into deeper and deeper levels of solidity. You eliminate unnecessary tension and stress in your focus, finding ways of feeling more and more at home, at ease, in the experience of the present.

Once the mind is settled down, give it time to stay there. Don't be in too great a hurry to move on. Here the questions are, "Which parts of the process were necessary to focus in? Which can now be let go? Which do you have to hold onto in order to maintain this focus?" Tuning into the right level of awareness is one process; staying there is another. When you learn how to maintain your sense of stillness, try to keep it going in all situations. What do you discover gets in the way? Is it your own resistance to disturbances? Can you make your stillness so porous so that disturbances can go through without running into anything, without knocking your center off balance?

As you get more and more absorbed in exploring these issues, concentration becomes less a battle against disturbance and more an opportunity for inner exploration. And without even thinking about them, you're developing the four bases of success: the desire to understand things, the persistence that keeps after your exploration, the close attention you're paying to cause and effect, and the ingenuity you're putting into framing the questions you ask. All these qualities contribute to concentration, help it get settled, get solid, get clear.

At the same time, they foster discernment. The Buddha once said that the test for a person's discernment is how he or she frames a question and tries to answer it. Thus to foster discernment, you can't simply stick to pre-set directions in your meditation. You have to give yourself practice in framing questions and testing the karma of those questions by looking for their results.

Ultimately, when you reach a perception of the breath that allows the sensations of in-and-out breathing to grow still, so you can start questioning more subtle perceptions of the body. It's like tuning into a radio station. If your receiver isn't precisely tuned to the frequency of the signal, the static interferes with the subtleties of whatever is being transmitted. But when you're precisely tuned, every nuance comes through. The same with your sensation of the body: when the movements of the breath grow still, the more subtle nuances of how perception interacts with physical sensation come to the fore. The body seems like a mist of atomic sensations, and you can begin to see how your perceptions interact with that mist. To what extent is the shape of the body inherent in the mist? To what extent is it intentional—something added? What happens when you drop the intention to create that shape? Can you focus on the space between the droplets in the mist? What happens then? Can you stay there? What happens when drop the perception of space and focus on the knowing? Can you stay there? What happens when you drop the oneness of the knowing? Can you stay there? What happens when you try to stop labeling anything at all?

As you settle into these more formless states, it's important that you not lose sight of your purpose in tuning into them. You're here to understand suffering, not to over-interpret what you experience. Say, for instance, that you settle into an enveloping sense of space or consciousness. From there, it's easy to assume that you've reached the primordial awareness, the ground of being, from which all things emerge, to which they all return, and which is essentially untouched by the whole process of emerging and returning. You might take descriptions of the Unconditioned and apply them to what you're experiencing. If you're abiding in a state of neither perception nor non-perception, it's easy to see it as a non-abiding, devoid of distinctions between perceiver and perceived, for mental activity is so attenuated as to be virtually imperceptible. Struck with the apparent effortless of the state, you may feel that you've gone beyond passion, aversion, and delusion simply by regarding them as unreal. If you latch onto an assumption like this, you can easily think that you've reached the end of the path before your work is really done.

Your only protection here is to regard these assumptions as forms of perception, and to dismantle them as well. And here is where the four noble truths prove their worth, as tools for dismantling any assumption by detecting the stress that accompanies it. Ask if there's still some subtle stress in the concentration that has become your dwelling place. What goes along with that stress? What vagrant movements in the mind are creating it? What persistent movements in the mind are creating it? You have to watch for both.

In this way you come face to face with the perceptions that keep even the most subtle states of concentration going. And you see that even *they* are stressful. If you replace them with other perceptions, though, you'll simply exchange one type of stress for another. It's as if your ascending levels of concentration have brought you to the top of a flag pole. You look down and see aging, illness, and death coming up the pole, in pursuit. You've exhausted all the options that perception can offer, so what are you going to do? You can't just stay where you are. Your only option is to release your grip. And if you're letting go fully, you let go of gravity, too.

The Weight of Mountains

Is a mountain heavy?

It may be heavy in and of itself, but as long as we don't try to lift it up, it won't be heavy for us.

This is a metaphor that one of my teachers, Ajaan Suwat, often used when explaining how to stop suffering from the problems of life. You don't deny their existence—the mountains *are* heavy—and you don't run away from them. As he would further explain, you deal with problems where you have to and solve them where you can. You simply learn how not to carry them around. That's where the art of the practice lies: in living with real problems without making their reality burden the heart.

As a beginning step in mastering that art, it's useful to look at the source for Ajaan Suwat's metaphor—the Buddha's teachings on *dukkha*—to get a fuller idea of how far the metaphor extends.

Dukkha is a word notoriously hard to translate into English. In the Pali canon, it applies both to physical and to mental pain and dis-ease, ranging from intense anguish to the subtlest sense of being burdened or confined. The Pali commentaries explain dukkha as "that which is hard to bear." Ajaan MahaBoowa, a Thai forest master, translates it as "whatever puts a squeeze on the heart." Although no single English term covers all of these meanings, the word "stress"—as a strain on body or mind—seems as close as English can get to the Pali term; "suffering" can be used in places where "stress" seems too mild.

The Buddha focused his teachings on the issue of stress because he had found a method for transcending it. To understand that method, we have to see which parts of our experience are marked by stress. From his perspective, experience falls into two broad categories: compounded (*saṅkhata*)—put together from causal forces and processes—and uncompounded (*asaṅkhata*). All ordinary experience is compounded. Even such a simple act as looking at a flower is compounded, in that it depends on the physical conditions supporting the flower's existence together with all the complex physical and mental factors

involved in the act of seeing. The only experience that isn't compounded is extraordinary—nirvana—for it doesn't depend on
causal factors of any kind.

Stress is totally absent from uncompounded experience. Its
relation to compounded experience, though, is more complex.
When the Buddha talked about dukkha in terms of the three
common characteristics—inconstancy, stress, and not-self—he
said that all compounded experiences are innately stressful.
From this point of view, even flower-gazing is stressful despite
the obvious pleasure it provides, for it relies on a fragile tension
among the combined factors making up the experience.

Thus if we want to go beyond stress we'll have to go beyond
compounded experience. But this presents a problem: what will
we use to reach the uncompounded? We can't use uncompounded experience to get us there, because—by definition—it
can't play a role in any causal process. It can't be used as a tool.
So we need a way of using compounded experience to tran-
scend itself.

To meet this need, the Buddha talked about dukkha in
another context: the four noble truths. Here, for strategic pur-
poses, he divided compounded experience into three
truths—stress, its cause (craving), and the way to its cessation
(the noble eightfold path). Uncompounded experience he left as
the remaining truth: the cessation of stress. In defining the first
truth he said that compounded experiences were stressful only
when accompanied by clinging. In this sense, flower-gazing
isn't stressful unless we cling to the experience and try to base
our happiness on it.

So it's obvious that in these two contexts the Buddha is
speaking of dukkha in two different senses. Ajaan Suwat's
mountain metaphor helps to explain how they are related. The
heaviness of the mountain stands for dukkha as a common characteristic: the stress inherent in all compounded experiences. The
fact that the mountain is heavy only for those who try to lift it
stands for dukkha as a noble truth: the stress that comes only
with clinging—the clinging that turns physical pain into mental
pain, and turns aging, illness, and death into mental distress.

The Buddha taught dukkha as a common characteristic to
make us reflect on the things we cling to: are they really worth
holding onto? If not, why keep holding on? If life offered no
pleasures better than those we already get from clinging, the

Buddha's insistence on the stress in things like flower-gazing might seem churlish and negative. But his purpose in getting us to reflect on the flip side of ordinary pleasures is to open our hearts to something very positive: the higher form of happiness, totally devoid of suffering and stress, that comes only with total letting go. So he also taught dukkha as a noble truth in order to focus our attention on where the real problem lies: not in the stressfulness of experiences, but in our ignorance in thinking we have to cling to them. And it's a good thing, too, that this is where the issue lies. As long as there are mountains, there's not much we can do about their inherent weight, but we can learn to break our habit of lifting them up and carrying them around. We can learn to stop clinging. That will put an end to our sufferings.

To understand how to let go effectively, it's helpful to look at the Pali word for clinging—*upādāna*—for it has a second meaning as well: the act of taking sustenance, as when a plant takes sustenance from the soil, or a fire from its fuel. This second meaning for upadana applies to the mind as well. When the mind clings to an object, it's feeding on that object. It's trying to gain nourishment from sensory pleasures, possessions, relationships, recognition, status, whatever, to make up for the gnawing sense of emptiness it feels inside. Unfortunately, this mental nourishment is temporary at best, so we keep hungering for more. Yet no matter how much the mind may try to possess and control its food sources to guarantee a constant supply, they inevitably break down. The mind is then burdened with searching for new places to feed.

So the issue of stress comes down to the feeding habits of the mind. If the mind didn't have to feed, it wouldn't suffer. At the same time, it would no longer create hardships for the people and things it consumes—through possession and control—as food. If we want to end suffering for ourselves and at the same time relieve the hardships of others, we thus have to strengthen the mind to the point where it doesn't have to feed, and then sharpen its discernment so that it doesn't *want* to feed. When it neither needs nor wants to feed, it will let go without our having to tell it to.

The practice to end dukkha would be quick and easy if we could simply go straight for the discernment that puts an end to clinging. The feeding analogy, though, helps to explain why simply seeing the drawbacks of clinging isn't enough to make us let go. If we're not strong enough to go without sustenance, the mind will keep finding new ways to feed and cling. So we first have to learn healthy feeding habits that will strengthen the mind. Only then will it be in a position where it no longer needs to feed.

How does the mind feed and cling? The Pali canon lists four ways:

(1) clinging to sensual passion for sights, sounds, smells, tastes, and tactile sensations;

(2) clinging to views about the world and the narratives of our lives;

(3) clinging to precepts and practices—i.e., fixed ways of doing things; and

(4) clinging to doctrines of the self—i.e., ideas of whether or not we have a true identity, or of what that identity might be.

There's rarely a moment when the ordinary mind isn't clinging in at least one of these ways. Even when we abandon one form of clinging, it's usually in favor of another. We may abandon a puritanical view because it interferes with sensual pleasure; or a sensual pleasure because it conflicts with a view about what we should do to stay healthy and fit. Our view of who we are may vary depending on which of our many senses of "I" is most pained, expanding into a sense of cosmic oneness when we feel confined by our small mind-body complex; and contracting into a small shell when we feel wounded from identifying with a cosmos so filled with cruelty and waste. When the insignificance of our finite self becomes oppressive again, we may jump at the idea that we have no self, but then *that* becomes oppressive.

So our minds jump from clinging to clinging like a bird trapped in a cage. When we realize we're captive, we naturally search for a way out, but everywhere we turn seems to be another side of the cage. We may begin to wonder whether there *is* a way out, or whether talk of full release is simply an old archetypal ideal that has nothing to do with human reality. But the Buddha was a great strategist: he realized that one of the walls of the cage is actually a door, and that if we grasp it skillfully, it'll swing wide open.

In other words, he found that the way to go beyond clinging is to turn our four ways of clinging into the path to their own abandoning. We'll need a certain amount of sensory pleasure—in terms of adequate food, clothing, and shelter—to find the strength to go beyond sensual passion. We'll need right view—seeing all things, including views, in terms of the four noble truths—to undermine our clinging to views. And we'll need a regimen of the five ethical precepts and the practice of meditation to put the mind in a solid position where it can drop its clinging to precepts and practices. Underlying all this, we'll need a healthy sense of self-love, self-responsibility, and self-discipline to master the practices leading to the insight that cuts through our clinging to doctrines of the self.

So we start the path to the end of suffering, not by trying to drop our clingings immediately, but by learning to cling more strategically. In terms of the feeding analogy, we don't try to starve the mind. We simply change its diet, weaning it away from junk food in favor of health food, developing inner qualities that will make it so strong that it won't need to feed ever again.

The canon lists these qualities as five:

> *conviction* in the principle of karma—that our happiness
>   depends on our own actions;
> *persistence* in abandoning unskillful qualities and developing
>   skillful ones in their stead;
> *mindfulness;*
> *concentration;* and
> *discernment.*

Of these, concentration—at the level of *jhāna,* or intense absorption—is the strength that the Buddhist tradition most often compares to good, healthy food. A discourse in the Aṅguttara Nikaya (VII.63) compares the four levels of jhana to the provisions used to stock a frontier fortress. Ajaan Lee, one of the Thai forest masters, compares them to the provisions needed on a journey through a lonely, desolate forest. Or as Dhammapada 200 says about the rapture of jhana,

> *How very happily we live,*
> *we who have nothing.*
> *We will feed on rapture*
> *   like the Radiant gods.*

As for discernment: When the mind is strengthened with the food of good concentration, it can begin contemplating the drawbacks of having to feed. This is the part of the Buddha's teaching that—for many of us—goes most directly against the grain, because feeding, in every sense of the word, is our primary way of relating to and enjoying the world around us. Our most cherished sense of inter-connectedness with the world—what some people call our interbeing—is, at its most basic level, inter-eating. We feed on others, and they feed on us. Sometimes our relationships are mutually nourishing, sometimes not, but either way it's hard to imagine any lasting relationship where some kind of physical or mental nourishment wasn't being consumed. At the same time, feeding is the activity in which we experience the most intimate sense of ourselves. We define ourselves through the pleasures, people, ideas, and activities we keep returning to for nourishment.

So it's hard for us to imagine a world, any possibility of enjoyment—even our very self—where we wouldn't inter-eat. Our common resistance to the idea of no longer feeding—one of the Buddha's most radically uncommon teachings—comes largely from a failure of the imagination. We can hardly conceive of what he's trying to tell us. So he has to prescribe some strong medicine to jog our minds into new perspectives.

This is where his teachings on dukkha, or stress, come into play. When the mind is strong and well fed, it can begin to look objectively at the stress involved in having to feed. The teachings on dukkha as a common characteristic focus on the drawbacks of what the mind takes for food. Sometimes it latches onto out-and-out suffering. It clings to the body even when racked with pain. It clings to its preferences and relationships even when these bring anguish, grief, and despair. Sometimes the mind latches onto pleasures and joys, but pleasures and joys turn stressful when they deteriorate and change. In any event, *everything* the mind latches onto is by its very nature compounded, and there's always at least a subtle level of stress inherent in keeping the compound going. This applies not only to gross, external conditions, but even to the most subtle levels of concentration in the mind.

When we see stress as a characteristic common to all the things we latch onto, it helps dispel their allure. Pleasures begin to ring hollow and false. Even our sufferings—which we can often glamorize with a perverse pride—begin to seem banal when reduced to their common characteristic of stress. This helps cut them down to size.

Of course, some people object to the idea of contemplating the dukkha inherent in the mind's food, on the grounds that this contemplation doesn't do justice to the many joys and satisfactions in

life. The Buddha, however, never denies the existence of pleasure. He simply points out that if you focus on the allure of your
food, you'll never be able to outgrow your eating addictions. It
would be like asking an alcoholic to muse on the subtle good
flavors of scotch and wine.

Dukkha is inherent not only in the things on which we feed, but
also in the very act of feeding. This is the focal point for the
Buddha's teaching on dukkha as a noble truth. If we have to feed,
we're a slave to our appetites. And can we trust ourselves to behave
in honorable ways when the demands of these slave drivers aren't
met? Inter-eating is not always a pretty thing. At the same time, as
long as we need to feed we're prey to any uncertainties in our food
sources, at the mercy of any people or forces with power over them.
If we can't do without them, we're chained to them. The mind isn't
free to go places where there isn't any food. And, as the Buddha
guarantees, those are precisely the places—beyond our ordinary
mental horizons—where the greatest happiness lies.

The purpose of these two contemplations—on the stress
inherent both in the mind's food and in the way it feeds—is to
sensitize us to limitations that we otherwise accept, sometimes
blithely, always blindly, without thought. Once the realization
finally hits home that they're not worth the price they entail, we
lose all infatuation with our desire to feed. And, unlike the body,
the mind can reach a level of strength where it no longer needs
to cling or take in sustenance, even from the path of practice.
When it becomes strong enough in conviction, persistence,
mindfulness, concentration, and discernment, it can open to a
dimension—the deathless—where there is neither feeding nor
being fed upon. That puts an end to the "feeder," and there's no
more suffering with regard to food. In other words, once we've
fully penetrated the deathless, dukkha as a common characteristic is no longer an issue; dukkha as a noble truth no longer exists.

This is where you discover something unexpected: the
mountains you've been trying to lift are all a by-product of your
feeding. When you stop feeding, no new mountains are formed.
Although there may still be some past-karma mountains
remaining around you, they'll eventually wear away and no
new ones will take their place. In the meantime, their weight is
no longer a problem. Once you've finally stopped trying to lift
them up, there's nothing to hold you down.

Five Piles of Bricks

The Khandhas as Burden & Path

The Buddha's Awakening gave him, among other things, a new perspective on the uses and limitations of words. He had discovered a reality—the Deathless—that no words could describe. At the same time, he discovered that the path to Awakening *could* be described, although it involved a new way of seeing and conceptualizing the problem of suffering and stress. Because ordinary concepts were often poor tools for teaching the path, he had to invent new concepts and to stretch pre-existing words to encompass those concepts so that others could taste Awakening themselves.

One of the new concepts most central to his teaching was that of the *khandhas*, which are most frequently translated into English as "aggregates." Prior to the Buddha, the Pali word *khandha* had very ordinary meanings: A khandha could be a pile, a bundle, a heap, a mass. It could also be the trunk of a tree. In his first sermon, though, the Buddha gave it a new, psychological meaning, introducing the term "clinging-khandhas" to summarize his analysis of the truth of stress and suffering. Throughout the remainder of his teaching career, he referred to these psychological khandhas time and again. Their importance in his teachings has thus been obvious to every generation of Buddhists ever since. Less obvious, though, has been the issue of *how* they are important: How should a meditator make use of the concept of the psychological khandhas? What questions are they meant to answer?

The most common response to these questions is best exemplified by two recent scholarly books devoted to the subject. Both treat the khandhas as the Buddha's answer to the question, "What is a person?" To quote from the jacket of the first:

"If Buddhism denies a permanent self, how does it perceive identity? ... What we conventionally call a 'person' can be understood in terms of five aggregates, the sum of which must not be taken for a permanent entity, since

beings are nothing but an amalgam of ever-changing
phenomena.... [W]ithout a thorough understanding of
the five aggregates, we cannot grasp the liberation
process at work within the individual, who is, after all,
simply an amalgam of the five aggregates."

From the introduction of the other:

"The third key teaching is given by the Buddha in contexts when he is asked about individual identity: when
people want to know 'what am I?', 'what is my *real*
self?'. The Buddha says that individuality should be
understood in terms of a combination of phenomena
which appear to form the physical and mental contin-
uum of an individual life. In such contexts, the human
being is analysed into five constituents—the *pañ-
cakkhandha* [five aggregates]."

This understanding of the khandhas isn't confined to scholars. Almost any modern Buddhist meditation teacher would
explain the khandhas in a similar way. And it isn't a modern
innovation. It was first proposed at the beginning of the
common era in the commentaries to the early Buddhist
canons—both the Theravadin and the Sarvastivadin, which
formed the basis for Mahayana scholasticism.

However, once the commentaries used the khandhas to
define what a person is, they spawned many of the controversies that have plagued Buddhist thinking ever since: "If a
person is just khandhas, then what gets reborn?" "If a person is
just khandhas, and the khandhas are annihilated on reaching
total nibbana, then isn't total nibbana the annihilation of the
person?" "If a person is khandhas, and khandhas are interrelated with other khandhas, how can one person enter nibbana
without dragging everyone else along?"

A large part of the history of Buddhist thought has been the
story of ingenious but unsuccessful attempts to settle these
questions. It's instructive to note, though, that the Pali canon
never quotes the Buddha as trying to answer them. In fact, it
never quotes him as trying to define what a person is at all.
Instead, it quotes him as saying that to define yourself in any
way is to limit yourself, and that the question, "What am I?" is
best ignored. This suggests that he formulated the concept of
the khandhas to answer other, different questions. If, as medita-

tors, we want to make the best use of this concept, we should look at what those original questions were, and determine how they apply to our practice.

The canon depicts the Buddha as saying that he taught only two topics: suffering and the end of suffering. A survey of the Pali discourses shows him using the concept of the khandhas to answer the primary questions related to those topics: What is suffering? How is it caused? What can be done to bring those causes to an end?

The Buddha introduced the concept of the khandhas in his first sermon in response to the first of these questions. His short definition of suffering was "the five clinging-khandhas." This fairly cryptic phrase can be fleshed out by drawing on other passages in the canon.

The five khandhas are bundles or piles of form, feeling, perception, fabrications, and consciousness. None of the texts explain why the Buddha used the word khandha to describe these things. The meaning of "tree trunk" may be relevant to the pervasive fire imagery in the canon—nibbana being extinguishing of the fires of passion, aversion, and delusion—but none of the texts explicitly make this connection. The common and explicit image is of the khandhas as burdensome. We can think of them as piles of bricks we carry on our shoulders. However, these piles are best understood, not as objects, but as activities, for an important passage defines them in terms of their functions. Form—which covers physical phenomena of all sorts, both within and without the body—wears down or "de-forms." Feeling feels pleasure, pain, and neither pleasure nor pain. Perception labels or identifies objects. Consciousness cognizes the six senses (counting the intellect as the sixth) along with their objects. Of the five khandhas, fabrication is the most complex. Passages in the canon define it as intention, but it includes a wide variety of activities, such as attention, evaluation, and all the active processes of the mind. It is also the most fundamental khandha, for its primary activity is to take the potential for the experience of form, feeling, etc.—coming from past actions— and turn it into the actual experience of those things in the present moment.

Thus intention is an integral part of our experience of all the khandhas—an important point, for this means that there is an element of intention in all suffering. This opens the possibility that suffering can be ended by changing our intentions—or abandoning them entirely—which is precisely the point of the Buddha's teachings.

To understand how this happens, we have to look more closely at how suffering arises—or, in other words, how khandhas become clinging-khandhas.

When khandhas are experienced, the process of fabrication normally doesn't simply stop there. If attention focuses on the khandhas' attractive features—beautiful forms, pleasant feelings, etc.—it can give rise to passion and delight. This passion and delight can take many forms, but the most tenacious is the habitual act of fabricating a sense of me or mine, identifying with a particular khandha (or set of khandhas) or claiming possession of it.

This sense of me and mine is rarely static. It roams like an ameba, changing its contours as it changes location. Sometimes expansive, sometimes contracted, it can view itself as identical with a khandha, as possessing a khandha, as existing within a khandha, or as having a khandha existing within itself. At times feeling finite, at other times infinite, whatever shape it takes it's always unstable and insecure, for the khandhas providing its food are simply activities and functions, inconstant and insubstantial. In the words of the canon, the khandhas are like foam, like a mirage, like the bubbles formed when rain falls on water. They're heavy only because the iron grip of trying to cling to them is burdensome. As long as we're addicted to passion and delight for these activities—as long as we cling to them—we're bound to suffer.

The Buddhist approach to ending this clinging, however, is not simply to drop it. As with any addiction, the mind has to be gradually weaned away. Before we can reach the point of no intention, where we're totally freed from the fabrication of khandhas, we have to change our intentions toward the khandhas so as to change their functions. Instead of using them for the purpose of constructing a self, we use them for the purpose of creating a path to the end of suffering. Instead of carrying piles of bricks on our shoulders, we take them off and lay them along the ground as pavement.

The first step in this process is to use the khandhas to construct the factors of the noble eightfold path. For example, Right Concentration: We maintain a steady perception focused on an aspect of form, such as the breath, and used directed thought and evaluation—which count as fabrications—to create feelings of pleasure and refreshment, which we spread through the body. In the beginning, it's normal that we experience passion and delight for these feelings, and that consciousness follows along in line with them. This helps get us absorbed in mastering the skills of concentration.

Once we've gained the sense of strength and wellbeing that comes from mastering these skills, we can proceed to the second step: attending to the drawbacks of even the refined khandhas we experience in concentration, so as to undercut the passion and delight we might feel for them:

> "Suppose that an archer or archer's apprentice were to practice on a straw man or mound of clay, so that after a while he would become able to shoot long distances, to fire accurate shots in rapid succession, and to pierce great masses. In the same way, there is the case where a monk...enters & remains in the first jhana: rapture & pleasure born of withdrawal, accompanied by directed thought & evaluation. He regards whatever phenomena there that are connected with form, feeling, perceptions, fabrications, & consciousness, as inconstant, stressful, a disease, a cancer, an arrow, painful, an affliction, alien, a disintegration, a void, not-self. [Similarly with the other levels of jhana.]"

The various ways of fostering dispassion are also khandhas, khandhas of perception. A standard list includes the following: the perception of inconstancy, the perception of not-self, the perception of unattractiveness, the perception of drawbacks (the diseases to which the body is subject), the perception of abandoning, the perception of distaste for every world, the perception of the undesirability of all fabrications. One of the most important of these perceptions is that of not-self. When the Buddha first introduced the concept of not-self in his second sermon, he also introduced a way of strengthening its impact with a series of questions based around the khandhas. Taking each khandha in turn, he asked: "Is it constant or inconstant?" Inconstant. "And is what is inconstant stressful or pleasurable?" Stressful. "And is it fitting to regard what is inconstant, stressful, subject to change as: 'This is mine. This is my self. This is what I am'?" No.

These questions show the complex role the khandhas play in this second step of the path. The questions themselves are khandhas—of fabrication—and they use the concept of the khandhas to deconstruct any passion and delight that might center on the khandhas and create suffering. Thus, in this step, we use khandhas that point out the drawbacks of the khandhas.

If used unskillfully, though, these perceptions and fabrications can simply replace passion with its mirror image, aversion. This is why they have to be based on the first step—the wellbeing constructed in jhana—and coupled with the third step, the perceptions of dispassion and cessation that incline the mind to the deathless: "This is peace, this is exquisite—the resolution of all fabrications; the relinquishment of all acquisitions; the ending of craving; dispassion; cessation; Unbinding." In effect, these are perception-khandhas that point the mind beyond all khandhas.

The texts say that this three-step process can lead to one of two results. If, after undercutting passion and delight for the khandhas, the mind contains any residual passion for the perception of the deathless, it will attain the third level of Awakening, called non-return. If passion and delight are entirely eradicated, though, all clinging is entirely abandoned, the intentions that fabricate khandhas are dropped, and the mind totally released. The bricks of the pavement have turned into a runway, and the mind has taken off.

Into what? The authors of the discourses seem unwilling to say, even to the extent of describing it as a state of existence, non-existence, neither, or both. As one of the discourses states, the freedom lying beyond the khandhas also lies beyond the realm to which language properly applies. There is also the very real practical problem that any preconceived notions of that freedom, if clung to as a perception-khandha, could easily act as an obstacle to its attainment. Still, there is also the possibility that, if properly used, such a perception-khandha might act as an aid on the path. So the discourses provide hints in the form of similes, referring to total freedom as:

> *The unfashioned, the end,*
> *the effluent-less, the true, the beyond,*
> *the subtle, the very-hard-to-see,*
> *the ageless, permanence, the undecaying,*

the featureless, non-elaboration,
peace, the deathless,
the exquisite, bliss, solace,
the exhaustion of craving,
the wonderful, the marvelous,
the secure, security,
unbinding,
the unafflicted, the passionless, the pure,
release, non-attachment,
the island, shelter, harbor, refuge,

the ultimate.

Other passages mention a consciousness in this freedom—
"without feature or surface, without end, luminous all
around"—lying outside of time and space, experienced when
the six sense spheres stop functioning. In this it differs from the
consciousness-khandha, which depends on the six sense
spheres and can be described in such terms as near or far, past,
present, or future. Consciousness without feature is thus the
awareness of Awakening. And the freedom of this awareness
carries over even when the awakened person returns to ordinary consciousness. As the Buddha said of himself:

> "Freed, dissociated, & released from form, the Tathagata
> dwells with unrestricted awareness. Freed, dissociated,
> & released from feeling ... perception ... fabrications ...
> consciousness ... birth ... aging ... death ... suffering &
> stress ... defilement, the Tathagata dwells with unre-
> stricted awareness."

This shows again the importance of bringing the right questions to the teachings on the khandhas. If you use them to
define what you are as a person, you tie yourself down to no
purpose. The questions keep piling on. But if you use them to
put an end to suffering, your questions fall away and you're
free. You never again cling to the khandhas and no longer need
to use them to end your self-created suffering. As long as you're
still alive, you can employ the khandhas as needed for whatever
skillful uses you see fit. After that, you're liberated from all uses
and needs, including the need to find words to describe that
freedom to yourself or to anyone else.

Perennial Issues

Perennial philosophers—those who assert the existence of a perennial philosophy—base their thinking on two claims. The first is a fact-claim: all the great religious traditions of the world share a common core of beliefs. The second is a value-claim: the commonality of these beliefs is proof that they are true.

The idea of such a perennial philosophy is attractive. It suggests a way of arriving at religious truths that are universal and objective, rather than culturally conditioned. It offers a plot of common ground where different religions, instead of fighting over their differences, can live in harmony and peace. In fact, some perennial philosophers maintain that the objectivity of perennial philosophy makes it so scientifically respectable that it can provide the framework by which all human knowledge—spiritual and scientific—can be brought together in an overarching theory that allots to each body of knowledge its proper function and place.

However, there are problems with both of the claims on which perennial philosophy is based—problems that undermine the validity of the perennial philosophers' project and deflect their attention from more important issues that any quest for spiritual objectivity should address.

The problems with the fact-claim derive from the methodology used for establishing the common core of the great traditions. The primary question tackled by the perennial philosophy, we are told, is that of our true identity—"What is my true self?"—and the answer to that question is that our true self is identical with Being as a whole. We are all One, and our common identity extends to the source of all things. To arrive at this answer, though, the perennial philosophers have had to discount many of the teachings—found in most of the world's major religions—that posit a separate identity for each person, and a creator of the universe separate from its creation.

To get around this difficulty, perennial philosophers have tried to limit the range of what they mean by a "great religious tradition." They draw the line around this concept in one of two ways. The first is to draw a distinction, inherited from the Romantics, between conventional religious doctrines and the insights of direct religious or mystical experience. Mystical experience is the direct apprehension of inner truths. Conventional doctrines are the corruption of those truths, formulated by people of a lower level of religious inspiration, influenced by social, cultural, or political factors. Thus perennial philosophers claim that they are justified in ignoring conventional doctrines and drawing their raw data only from reports of mystical experience, for these are closest to the truths of direct experience.

The problem here is that many accounts of direct religious experiences do not support the tenets of perennial philosophy. The Buddha's Awakening is a case in point. That Awakening obviously qualifies as a direct religious experience, and yet the descriptions of that experience found in the earliest records, the Pali canon, contain nothing to support the perennial philosophy's answer to the question of personal identity. They don't even address the question. In fact, there are passages in the Pali canon where the Buddha denounces questions of identity and being—"Who am I? What am I? Do I exist? Do I not exist?"—as inappropriate entanglements blocking the path to Awakening.

Perennial philosophers have tried to get around this difficulty in two ways. One is to cite the Pali texts but to re-interpret them. The teaching on not-self, they say, is simply an indirect way of approaching the basic tenet of perennial philosophy: if one abandons one's identification with the aggregates of the small self, one awakens to one's identity with the larger self: the Oneness of the All. Even though the Awakening account makes no mention of a larger self or of any feelings of oneness, the perennial philosophers assume by extrapolation from accounts in other traditions that they must have been present in the Buddha's experience, and that either he neglected to mention them or his followers dropped them from their records. The problem here is that the Pali canon assigns feelings of oneness to mundane levels of concentration, and not to the transcendent. It also lumps views of an infinite self in with views of a finite self as equally untenable. And even though the Pali canon admits that its description of the Buddha's Awakening is incomplete, there is no reason to believe that the unexpressed essence of his Awakening would be expressed with a tenet that he explicitly said to abandon.

This difficulty has led to a second way of dealing with the problem of the Pali canon: to dismiss it entirely in favor of Mahayana texts that fit better with the tenets of perennial philosophy. Rather than treating Theravada Buddhism as a tradition with its own integrity, perennial philosophers adopt the Mahayana polemical stance: that Theravada, despite its claims to being a complete tradition, is simply an incomplete fragment of a tradition that finds its explicit completion only in the Mahayana itself.

The perennial philosophers' reasons for adopting this stance relate to the second way in which they delimit the meaning of "great religious tradition": the implicit value-claim that non-dualism is superior to dualism or pluralism. The superiority of non-dualism, they say, is both conceptual and ethical. Conceptually it is more inclusive, encompassing a larger view. The erasing of distinctions is superior to the creation of distinctions. Ethically, non-dualism leads to acts of kindness and compassion: when people sense their essential oneness, they are more likely to treat one another with the same care they would treat themselves. Thus the great religious traditions must, by definition, be non-dualistic.

Both the conceptual and the ethical arguments for non-dualism, however, are open to question. Conceptually, there is no proof that a non-dual view is necessarily more encompassing that a dual or pluralistic view. A person who has had a direct experience of duality may have touched something that lies outside the oneness comprehended by the non-dualist. The Pali interpretation of nirvana is an example: nirvana lies outside the oneness of jhana, and even the Allness of the All—the entire range of the six senses (including the mind) and their objects. And it does not include them. Secondly, there are many areas of life in which distinctions are clearly superior to a lack of distinctions. When you need brain surgery, you want a doctor who is clear about the distinction between skillful and unskillful methods. A person who sees distinctions may be detecting subtle differences that a non-dualist simply hasn't noticed.

Ethically, the superiority of non-dualism is even harder to prove. To begin with, the notion of ethical superiority is in and of itself a dualistic position: if compassion is better than cruelty, there has to be a distinction between the two. Secondly, there is the problem of theodicy, the explanation for the source of evil in a just universe. If all things come from one source, where does evil come from? One common non-dualist answer is that it comes from ignorance of our essential oneness, but that simply drives the question back another step: where does ignorance come from, if not from the One Source? How can the One Source be ignorant of itself? Is it incompetent? Is it playing an inhumane game?

This issue of theodicy has been argued repeatedly over the ages in every tradition that posits a single source for the cosmos, and the non-dualist answers eventually come down to three: evil is either illusory or necessary or both. But if you can say that evil is illusory, it's a sign that you've never been victimized by evil. If you say that it's necessary, then what incentive is there for people not to do it? Those who want to do evil can simply say that they're performing a necessary function in the world. This point is illustrated by the Indian legend of the murderer who met a philosophical non-dualist on the road and challenged him to give one reason, consistent with his philosophy, for why he shouldn't allow himself to be stabbed. The non-dualist was unable to do so, and so he met his death.

Thus it's apparent that the fact-claim of perennial philosophy—that it is giving voice to the essential message of all the world's great religious traditions—depends on a very restricted definition of "all." The great religious traditions are by definition those who agree with its principles. Those who don't are lesser traditions and so may be discounted. This means that the perennial philosophers' comments about "all great religions" are not simple observations about a range of phenomena whose boundaries are already widely accepted. Instead, they're an attempt to define those boundaries—and a very exclusionary one at that. There's no way that such a restricted vision of the world's religious traditions could provide a rallying point that would unite them in peace and harmony. It simply adds one more divisive voice to the clamor.

However, even if the fact-claim of a perennial philosophy were better based, there would still be reason to question its value-claim: that consensus is proof of truth. Even if the great traditions did share a common core of beliefs, that would be no guarantee of its validity. No reputable body of knowledge has ever viewed simple consensus as proof of a proposition's truth. The history of science is littered with truths that were once universally accepted and now no longer are. It's also studded with stories of ideas that were originally rejected because they bucked the consensus but later were established as true. This shows that consensus is not proof. If valid, it follows on proof. And the standards for proof are to be sought in the story of how one truth overthrows another. Invariably, as we read through history, we find that this happens because the new truth is better in one of two ways: either in terms of the method used to arrive at or in terms of its uses, the beneficial actions it inspires. Galileo's ideas on matter and acceleration were accepted over Aristotle's because they were based on better experiments. Newton's, and not Aristotle's, are still used by NASA because they have been found more useful in getting rockets to Mars.

This historical fact suggests that truth-claims are established, not by consensus, but by human activity: the actions that lead to the discovery of truths and those that result from their acceptance. And if ever there were an issue that a scientific inquiry into religion should address, this is it: How should the relation between truth and activity best be understood, and how should it be applied to greatest advantage? If this issue is not addressed, how can we know what to do to find truths, or what to do with them once they're found?

So far, however, perennial philosophers have had nothing to say on this topic. In fact, they repeatedly state that the question of which methods—or non-methods—the great religious have used to arrive at their consensus is immaterial. All that matters is that they agree. But what if all those methods were questionable? And what if their consensus creates more problems than it solves? As we have already noted, the non-dualistic stance proposed by the perennial philosophers, if carefully questioned, has trouble speaking to the reality of evil or providing an incentive against doing it. Thus they fail both tests for verifying truths: they are non-committal on the issue of what actions are needed to discover spiritual truths, and the propose a truth that unwittingly opens the door to evil actions that would result from accepting their claims.

So, given the weaknesses in the fact-claims and value-claims on which perennial philosophy is based, does that mean that the quest for objective spiritual truths is doomed to failure? Not necessarily. It simply means that the perennial philosophers have been asking the wrong questions and using a faulty methodology to answer them. A more fruitful line of inquiry would be to focus on the spiritual implications of the question raised above: How should the relation between truth and activity best be understood, and how should it be applied to greatest advantage? This question lies at the basis of the scientific method, so any scientific account of religion would have to begin here. This study could start by searching the religious traditions of the world, not for their fact-statements, but for their statements on what actions are needed to verify facts. These truth/action claims could then be compared and put to the test.

And this is an area where the Pali canon has a great deal to say. Its descriptions of the Buddha's Awakening—focusing on karma, causality, and the four noble truths—directly address the question of how truth and activity are related. The Buddha's realizations concerning karma and causality focus on the way beliefs and actions influence one another. His insights into the four noble truths focus on the way karma and causality can best be put to use to bring an end to suffering. His Awakening provided answers to the questions of (1) what action is, (2) what the highest happiness is that action can produce, (3) what beliefs lead to the most skillful actions, and (4) what actions can provide an adequate test for those beliefs.

Furthermore, the Pali canon contains explicit instructions on how the Buddha's teachings are to be tested by others. His famous instructions to the Kalamas, that they should know for themselves, are accompanied by detailed standards—unfortunately, considerably less famous—on what procedures any valid "knowing for oneself" should entail.

Whether the canon's answers to these questions are adequate and convincing may be subject to debate. But they provide a clear starting point for exploring the issue of what to *do* with fact-claims and value-claims: the first issue that any objective inquiry into spiritual truths should address.

"When you know for yourselves ..."

The Authenticity of the Pali Suttas

The Theravada tradition, dominant in Sri Lanka, Myanmar, and Thailand, regards the Pali suttas as the authentic and authoritative record of the Buddha's own words. When Western scholars—piqued by issues of authority and authenticity—first learned of these claims in the 19th century, they began employing the historical method to test them. And although every conceivable scrap of literary or archeological evidence seems to have been examined, no air-tight historical proof or disproof of these claims has surfaced. What *has* surfaced is a mass of minor facts and probabilities—showing that the Pali canon is *probably* the closest detailed record we have of the Buddha's teachings—but nothing more certain than that. Archeological evidence shows that Pali was probably not the Buddha's native language, but is this proof that he didn't use Pali when talking to native speakers of that language? The canon contains grammatical irregularities, but are these signs of an early stage in the language, before it was standardized, or a later stage of degeneration? And in which stage of the language's development did the Buddha's life fall? Fragments of other early Buddhist canons have been found, with slight deviations from the Pali canon in their wording, but not in their basic doctrines. Is their unanimity in doctrine a sign that they all come from the Buddha himself, or was it the product of a later conspiracy to remake and standardize the doctrine in line with changed beliefs and tastes? Scholars have proven eager to take sides on these issues, but the inevitable use of inference, conjecture, and probabilities in their arguments lends an air of uncertainty to the whole process.

Many have seen this uncertainty as sign of the inadequacy of the Theravadin claims to authenticity. But simply to dismiss the teachings of the suttas for this reason would be to deprive ourselves of the opportunity to test their most remarkable assertion: that human effort, properly directed, can put an end to all suffering and stress. Perhaps we should instead question the methods of the historians, and view the uncertainty of their conclusions as a sign of the inadequacy of the historical method as a tool for ascertaining the Dhamma. The suttas themselves make this point in their own recommendations for how the authenticity and authority of the Dhamma is best ascertained. In a famous passage, they quote the Buddha as saying:

> "Kalamas, don't go by reports, by legends, by traditions, by scripture, by logical conjecture, by inference, by analogies, by agreement through pondering views, by probability, or by the thought, 'This contemplative is our teacher.' When you know for yourselves that, 'These dhammas are unskillful; these dhammas are blameworthy; these dhammas are criticized by the wise; these dhammas, when adopted and carried out, lead to harm and to suffering'—then you should abandon them .... When you know for yourselves that, 'These dhammas are skillful; these dhammas are blameless; these dhammas are praised by the wise; these dhammas, when adopted and carried out, lead to welfare and to happiness'—then you should enter and remain in them."

AN III.66

Because this passage is contained in a religious scripture, the statements attracting the most attention have been those rejecting the authority of religious teachers, legends, traditions, and scripture; along with those insisting on the importance of knowing for oneself. These remarkably anti-dogmatic statements— sometimes termed the Buddha's Charter of Free Inquiry—have tended to divert attention from the severe strictures that the passage places on what "knowing for oneself" entails. In questioning the authority of reports, it dismisses the basic material on which the historical method is based. In questioning the authority of inference and probability, it dismisses some of the method's basic techniques. In questioning the authority of logical conjecture, analogies, and agreement through pondering views, it dismisses the methods of free-thinking rationalism in general.

This leaves only two methods for ascertaining the Dhamma, both of them related to the question raised in this passage and central to other teachings in the canon: What is skillful, what is unskillful? In developing any skill, you must (1) pay attention to the results of your own actions; and (2) listen to those who have already mastered the skill. Similarly, in ascertaining the Dhamma, you must (1) examine the results that come for putting a particular teaching in practice; and (2) check those results against the opinions of the wise.

Two aspects of the Dhamma, however, make it a skill apart. The first is reflected in the fact that the word Dhamma means not only teaching, but also quality of the mind. Thus the above passage could also be translated:

> "When you know for yourselves that, 'These qualities are unskillful; these qualities are blameworthy; these qualities are criticized by the wise; these qualities, when adopted and carried out, lead to harm and to suffering'—then you should abandon them .... When you know for yourselves that, 'These qualities are skillful; these qualities are blameless; these qualities are praised by the wise; these qualities, when adopted and carried out, lead to welfare and to happiness'—then you should enter and remain in them."

In fact, this is more likely the correct translation, as the discussion following this passage focuses on the results of acting on qualities of the mind: greed, aversion, and delusion in the unskillful set; and lack of greed, lack of aversion, and lack of delusion in the skillful one. This points to the fact that Dhamma practice is primarily a skill of the *mind*.

The second aspect that sets the Dhamma apart as a skill is its goal: nothing less than the total ending of suffering.

While this second aspect of the Dhamma makes it an attractive skill to master, the first aspect makes it hard to determine who has mastered the skill and is thus qualified to speak about it with authority. After all, we can't look into the minds of others to see what qualities are there and what the internal results of the practice are. At best, we can detect hints of these things in their actions, but nothing more. Thus, if we look to others for the last word on the Dhamma, we will always be in a position of uncertainty. The only way to overcome uncertainty is to practice the Dhamma to see if it brings about an end to suffering within our own minds.

Traditionally, the texts state that uncertainty about the Dhamma ends only with the attainment of Stream-entry, the first of the four levels of Awakening. Even though a person who has reached this level of Awakening isn't totally immersed in the ending of suffering, he or she has seen enough of the end of suffering to know without a doubt that that's where the practice of the Dhamma leads. So it's not surprising that the four factors the suttas identify as bringing about Stream-entry are also the four methods they recommend for ascertaining whether they themselves are a truly authoritative and authentic guide to the end of suffering.

Those factors, listed in SN LV.5, are:

> association with people of integrity,
> listening to the true Dhamma,
> appropriate attention, and
> practice in accordance with the Dhamma.

Passages from the suttas dealing with each of these factors help show how the two sources of skill—the counsel of the wise and the lessons learned by observing the results of your own actions—can be properly balanced and integrated so as to ascertain what the true Dhamma is. And because listening to the true Dhamma now includes reading the true Dhamma, a knowledge of these factors and their interrelationships gives guidance in how to read the suttas. In particular, these factors show how the suttas themselves say they should be read, and what other actions provide the skillful context for getting the most benefit from reading them.

As you explore the explanations of these factors, you find that their presentation as a short list is deceptively simple, inasmuch as each factor contains elements of the other factors as well. For instance, associating with people of integrity is of great help in practicing the Dhamma, but for a person to recognize people of genuine integrity requires that he or she have some prior experience in practicing the Dhamma. Thus, although the form of the list suggests a simple linear progression, the individual factors of the list are interrelated in complex ways. What this means in practice is that the process of ascertaining the Dhamma is a complex one, requiring sensitivity and discernment in balancing and integrating the factors in an appropriate way.

Association with people of integrity. Because the Dhamma consists primarily of qualities of the mind, any written account of the Dhamma is only a pale shadow of the real thing. Thus, to gain a sense of the Dhamma's full dimensions, you must find people who embody the Dhamma in their thoughts, words, and deeds, and associate with them in a way that enables you to absorb as much of the Dhamma as possible. The passages explaining this factor thus offer advice in two areas: how to recognize people of integrity and how best to associate with them once you have found them.

The immediate sign of integrity is gratitude.

"A person of integrity is grateful and acknowledges the help given to him. This gratitude, this acknowledgment is second nature among admirable people. It is entirely on the level of people of integrity."

AN II.31

Gratitude is a necessary sign of integrity in that people who do *not* recognize and value the goodness and integrity in others are unlikely to make the effort to develop integrity within themselves. On its own, though, gratitude doesn't constitute integrity. The essence of integrity lies in three qualities: truth, harmlessness, and discernment.

"There is the case where a monk lives in dependence on a certain village or town. Then a householder or householder's son goes to him and observes him with regard to three mental qualities—qualities based on greed, qualities based on aversion, qualities based on delusion: 'Are there in this venerable one any such qualities based on greed ... aversion ... delusion that, with his mind overcome by these qualities, he might say, "I know," while not knowing, or say, "I see," while not seeing; or that he might urge another to act in a way that was for his/her long-term harm and pain?' As he observes him, he comes to know, 'There are in this venerable one no such qualities .... His bodily and verbal behavior are those of one not greedy ... aversive ... deluded. And the Dhamma he teaches is deep, hard to see, hard to realize, tranquil, refined, beyond the scope of conjecture, subtle, to-be-experienced by the wise."

MN 95

As this passage shows, knowledge of a person's truthfulness requires that you be so observant of his or her behavior that you can confidently infer the quality of his or her mind. This level of confidence, in turn, requires that you not only be observant, but also discerning and willing to take time, for as another passage points out, the appearance of spiritual integrity is easy to fake.

Then King Pasenadi Kosala went to the Blessed One and, on arrival, having bowed down to him, sat to one side. Then seven coiled-hair ascetics, seven Jain ascetics, seven naked ascetics, seven one-cloth ascetics, and seven wanderers—their nails grown long, their body-hair grown long—walked past not far from the Blessed One .... On seeing them, King Pasenadi arranged his upper robe over one shoulder, knelt down with his right knee on the ground, saluted the ascetics with his hands before his heart, and announced his name to them three times: "I am the king, venerable sirs, Pasenadi Kosala. I am the king, venerable sirs, Pasenadi Kosala. I am the king, venerable sirs, Pasenadi Kosala." Then not long after the ascetics had passed, he returned to the Blessed One and, on arrival, having bowed down to him, sat to one side. As he was sitting there he said to the Blessed One, "Of those in the world who are arahants or on the path to arahantship, are these among them?"

"Your majesty, as a layman enjoying sensual pleasures, living crowded with wives and children, using Kasi fabrics and sandalwood, wearing garlands, scents, and creams, handling gold and silver: it is hard for you to know whether these are arahants or on the path to arahantship.

"It's through living together that a person's virtue may be known, and then only after a long period, not a short period; by one who is attentive, not by one who is inattentive; by one who is discerning, not by one who isn't discerning.

"It's through trading with a person that his purity may be known ....

"It's through adversity that a person's endurance may be known ....

"It's through discussion that a person's discernment may be known, and then only after a long period, not a short period; by one who is attentive, not by one who is inattentive; by one who is discerning, not by one who isn't discerning."

"How amazing, lord! How awesome! How well that was put by the Blessed One! ... These men, lord, are my spies, my scouts, returning after going out through the countryside. They go out first, and then I go. Now, when they have scrubbed off the dirt and mud, are well-bathed and well-perfumed, have trimmed their hair and beards, and have put on white clothes, they will go about endowed and provided with the five strings of sensuality."

Ud VI.2

AN IV.192 expands on these points, indicating that the ability to recognize a person of integrity requires you to have a strong sense of integrity yourself. In fact, MN 110 insists that you must *be* a person of integrity in your actions, views, and friendships if you are to recognize integrity in another.

Listening to the True Dhamma. Once you've determined to the best of your ability that certain people embody integrity, the suttas advise listening to their Dhamma, both to learn *about* them—to further test their integrity—and to learn *from* them, to gain a sense of what the Dhamma might be. And again, the suttas recommend both how to listen to the Dhamma and how to recognize true Dhamma when you hear it.

MN 95 advises that you spend time near people of integrity, develop a sense of respect for them, and pay close attention to their Dhamma.

SN VI.2 and AN VIII.2 explain the purpose for respect here: it's a prerequisite for learning. Neither passage elaborates on this point, but its truth is fairly obvious. You find it easier to learn from someone you respect than from someone you don't.

Respect opens your mind and loosens your preconceived opinions to make room for new knowledge and skills. At the same
time, a person with a valuable teaching to offer will feel more
inclined to teach it to someone who shows respect than to someone who doesn't. However, respect doesn't necessarily mean
giving your full approval to the teaching. After all, part of the
purpose in listening to the Dhamma is to test whether the
person teaching it has integrity in his views or hers. Full
approval can come only when you've put the teaching in practice and tasted its results. This is why the Vinaya, the monastic
discipline, never requires that a student take vows of obedience
to a teacher. Here respect means, in the words of Sn II.9, a lack
of stubbornness. Or, in the words of AN VI.88, "the patience to
comply with the teaching": the willingness to listen with an
open mind and to take the time and effort needed to give any
teachings that seem reasonable a serious try.

The reasonability of the teaching can be gauged by the central principle in views of integrity as explained above in MN 110.
That principle is conviction in *kamma*, the efficacy of human
action: that people are responsible for their actions, that their
intentions determine the quality—the skillfulness or unskillfulness—of their actions, that actions give results, and that the
quality of the action determines the quality of the result. A
person who doesn't believe in these principles cannot be trusted.

Because the distinction between skillfulness and unskillfulness is central to the principle of kamma—and also to the
project of putting an end to suffering and stress—MN 135 recommends approaching potential teachers and asking them:

> "What is skillful? What is unskillful? What is blamewor-
> thy? What is blameless? What should be cultivated?
> What should not be cultivated? What, having been done
> by me, will be for my long-term harm and suffering? Or
> what, having been done by me, will be for my long-term
> welfare and happiness?"

The texts give a few examples of what might be called the
lowest common denominator for judging whether answers to
this question embody integrity. In essence, these teachings constitute "what works" in eliminating blatant levels of suffering
and stress in one's life.

"Now what is unskillful? Taking life is unskillful, taking what is not given...sexual misconduct...lying...abusive speech...divisive tale-bearing...idle chatter is unskillful. Covetousness...ill will...wrong views are unskillful. These things are termed unskillful.

"And what are the roots of unskillful things? Greed is a root of unskillful things, aversion is a root of unskillful things, delusion is a root of unskillful things. These are termed the roots of unskillful things.

"And what is skillful? Abstaining from taking life is skillful, abstaining from taking what is not given...from sexual misconduct...from lying...from abusive speech...from divisive tale-bearing...abstaining from idle chatter is skillful. Lack of covetousness...lack of ill will...right views are skillful. These things are termed skillful.

"And what are the roots of skillful things? Lack of greed is a root of skillful things, lack of aversion is a root of skillful things, lack of delusion is a root of skillful things. These are termed the roots of skillful things."

MN 9

"These three things have been promulgated by wise people, by people who are truly good. Which three? Generosity... going-forth [from the home life]... and service to one's mother and father. These three things have been promulgated by wise people, by people who are truly good."

AN III.45

However, the true Dhamma has a dimension that goes far beyond the lowest common denominator. To repeat the words of MN 95, it is "deep, hard to see, hard to realize, tranquil, refined, beyond the scope of conjecture, subtle, to-be-experienced by the wise." The principle of skillfulness—of cause and effect that can be tested in your own actions—still applies in this dimension, but the standards for "what works" on this level are correspondingly subtler and more refined. Two famous passages indicate what these standards are.

"Gotamı, the dhammas of which you may know, 'These dhammas lead—
>   to passion, not to dispassion;
>   to being fettered, not to being unfettered;
>   to accumulating, not to shedding;
>   to self-aggrandizement, not to modesty;
>   to discontent, not to contentment;
>   to entanglement, not to seclusion;
>   to laziness, not to aroused persistence;
>   to being burdensome, not to being unburdensome':
You may definitely hold, 'This is not the Dhamma, this is not the Vinaya, this is not the Teacher's instruction.'

"As for the dhammas of which you may know, 'These dhammas lead—
>   to dispassion, not to passion;
>   to being unfettered, not to being fettered;
>   to shedding, not to accumulating;
>   to modesty, not to self-aggrandizement;
>   to contentment, not to discontent;
>   to seclusion, not to entanglement;
>   to aroused persistence, not to laziness;
>   to being unburdensome, not to being burdensome':
You may definitely hold, 'This is the Dhamma, this is the Vinaya, this is the Teacher's instruction.'"

AN VIII.53

"Upali, the dhammas of which you may know, 'These dhammas do not lead to utter disenchantment, to dispassion, to cessation, to calm, to direct knowledge, to self-awakening, nor to Unbinding': You may definitely hold, 'This is not the Dhamma, this is not the Vinaya, this is not the Teacher's instruction.'

"As for the dhammas of which you may know, 'These dhammas lead to utter disenchantment, to dispassion, to cessation, to calm, to direct knowledge, to self-awakening, to Unbinding': You may definitely hold, 'This is the Dhamma, this is the Vinaya, this is the Teacher's instruction.'"

AN VII.80

AN VIII.30 expands on some of the principles in the first of
these two passages. But here we will focus on the points where
these two passages intersect—in the requirement that the
Dhamma lead to dispassion and to being unfettered—for the
standard test for a genuine experience of Awakening is that it
arises from dispassion and cuts the fetters of the mind.

"There are these ten fetters.... Self-identity views, uncertainty, grasping at precepts and practices, sensual desire,
and ill will. These are the five lower fetters. And which
are the five higher fetters? Passion for form, passion for
what is formless, conceit, restlessness, and ignorance.
These are the five higher fetters."

AN X.13

As MN 118 explains, stream-entry cuts the first three fetters;
once-returning, the second level of Awakening, weakens passion, aversion, and delusion; non-returning, the third level, cuts
the fetters of sensual desire and ill will; and arahantship, the
final level of Awakening, cuts the remaining five.

Ultimately, of course, the only proof for whether a teaching
leads in this direction comes when, having put the teaching into
practice, you actually begin to cut these fetters from the mind.
But as a preliminary exercise, you can contemplate a teaching to
make sense of it and to see if there are good reasons for believ-
ing that it will lead in the right direction.

"Hearing the Dhamma, one remembers it. Remembering
it, one penetrates the meaning of those dhammas.
Penetrating the meaning, one comes to an agreement
through pondering those dhammas. There being an
agreement through pondering those dhammas, desire
arises. With the arising of desire, one becomes willing.
Willing, one contemplates (lit: 'weighs,' 'compares')."

MN 95

The process of pondering, weighing, and comparing the
teachings is based on adopting the right attitude and asking the
right questions about them. As AN II.25 points out, some of the
teachings are meant to have their meaning inferred, whereas
others are not, and to misapprehend which of these two classes

a particular teaching belongs to is a serious mistake. This is where the next factor for stream-entry plays a role.

Appropriate attention. MN 2 draws the line between appropriate and inappropriate attention on the basis of the questions you choose to pursue in contemplating the Dhamma.

"There is the case where an uninstructed, run-of-the-mill person...doesn't discern what ideas are fit for attention, or what ideas are unfit for attention .... This is how he attends inappropriately: 'Was I in the past? Was I not in the past? What was I in the past? How was I in the past? Having been what, what was I in the past? Shall I be in the future? Shall I not be in the future? What shall I be in the future? How shall I be in the future? Having been what, what shall I be in the future?' Or else he is inwardly perplexed about the immediate present: 'Am I? Am I not? What am I? How am I? Where has this being come from? Where is it bound?'

"As he attends inappropriately in this way, one of six kinds of view arises in him: The view *I have a self* arises in him as true and established, or the view *I have no self...* or the view *It is precisely by means of self that I perceive self...* or the view *It is precisely by means of self that I perceive not-self...* or the view *It is precisely by means of not-self that I perceive self* arises in him as true and established, or else he has a view like this: *This very self of mine—the knower that is sensitive here and there to the ripening of good and bad actions—is the self of mine that is constant, everlasting, eternal, not subject to change, and will endure as long as eternity.* This is called a thicket of views, a wilderness of views, a contortion of views, a writhing of views, a fetter of views. Bound by a fetter of views, the uninstructed run-of-the-mill person is not freed from birth, aging, and death, from sorrow, lamentation, pain, distress, and despair. He is not freed, I tell you, from stress.

"The well-instructed disciple of the noble ones ...discerns what ideas are fit for attention, and what ideas are unfit for attention .... He attends appropriately, *This is stress... This is the origination of stress... This is the cessation of stress... This is the way leading to the cessation of stress.* As

he attends appropriately in this way, three fetters are
abandoned in him: self-identity views, doubt, and grasping at precepts and practices."

MN 2

Some of the most useless controversies in the history of
Buddhist thought have come from ignoring this teaching on
what is and is not an appropriate object for attention. Buddhists
have debated fruitlessly for centuries, and continue to debate
today, on how to define a person's identity—the answer to the
question, "What am I?"—or whether a person does or doesn't
have a self—the answer to the questions, "Am I? Am I not?"
The fruitlessness of these arguments has proven repeatedly the
point made by this passage: that any answer to these questions
leads to entanglement in the fetters that the Dhamma is meant
to cut away.

To avoid these controversies, the passage recommends
focusing on four truths that constitute the appropriate object for
attention—stress, its origination, its cessation, and the way leading to its cessation. These truths are directly related to the
question of skillfulness, which divides reality into two sets of
variables: cause and effect, skillful and unskillful. The origination of stress is an unskillful cause, and stress its result. The way
leading to the cessation of stress is a skillful cause, and the cessation of stress its result. To look at experience in these terms is
to attend appropriately in a way that can help cut the fetters
underlying unskillfulness in the mind.

For instance, SN LVI.11 defines the truth of stress as the five
clinging-aggregates—clinging to form, feeling, perception, fabrications, and consciousness—and maintains that this truth should
to be comprehended in such a way as to lead to dispassion for
the clinging. This, too, is a function of appropriate attention.

"A virtuous monk should attend in an appropriate way
to these five clinging-aggregates as inconstant, stressful,
a disease, a cancer, an arrow, painful, an affliction, alien,
a dissolution, an emptiness, not-self. For it is possible
that a virtuous monk, attending in an appropriate way
to these five clinging-aggregates as inconstant ... not-self,
would realize the fruit of stream-entry."

SN XXII.122

Thus appropriate attention entails a way of looking at the Dhamma not only as it is presented in a teaching, but also as it presents itself directly as experience to the mind.

Practice in accordance with the Dhamma. Once you've gained a sense of the Dhamma through appropriate attention, the remaining step is to practice in accordance with the Dhamma. As with the first two factors for stream-entry, this process is twofold: adapting your actions to follow in line with the Dhamma (rather than trying to adapt the Dhamma to follow your own preferences), and refining your understanding of the Dhamma as it is tested in experience.

MN 61 offers explicit instructions on how this is to be done.

"What do you think, Rahula: What is a mirror for?"

"For reflection, sir."

"In the same way, Rahula, bodily acts, verbal acts, and mental acts are to be done with repeated reflection.

"Whenever you want to perform a bodily act, you should reflect on it: 'This bodily act I want to perform— would it lead to self-affliction, to the affliction of others, or to both? Is it an unskillful bodily act, with painful consequences, painful results?' If, on reflection, you know that it would lead to self-affliction, to the affliction of others, or to both; it would be an unskillful bodily act with painful consequences, painful results, then any bodily act of that sort is absolutely unfit for you to do. But if on reflection you know that it would not cause affliction ... it would be a skillful bodily action with happy consequences, happy results, then any bodily act of that sort is fit for you to do.

"While you are performing a bodily act, you should reflect on it: 'This bodily act I am doing—is it leading to self-affliction, to the affliction of others, or to both? Is it an unskillful bodily act, with painful consequences, painful results?' If, on reflection, you know that it is leading to self-affliction, to affliction of others, or both ... you should give it up. But if on reflection you know that it is not ... you may continue with it.

"Having performed a bodily act, you should reflect on it
.... If, on reflection, you know that it led to self-affliction,
to the affliction of others, or to both; it was an unskillful
bodily act with painful consequences, painful results,
then you should confess it, reveal it, lay it open to the
Teacher or to a knowledgeable companion in the holy
life. Having confessed it ... you should exercise restraint
in the future. But if on reflection you know that it did
not lead to affliction... it was a skillful bodily action with
happy consequences, happy results, then you should
stay mentally refreshed and joyful, training day and
night in skillful mental qualities.

[Similarly for verbal acts and mental acts, although the
final paragraph concerning mental acts says:]

"Having performed a mental act, you should reflect on it
.... If, on reflection, you know that it led to self-affliction,
to the affliction of others, or to both; it was an unskillful
mental act with painful consequences, painful results,
then you should feel distressed, ashamed, and disgusted
with it. Feeling distressed ... you should exercise
restraint in the future. But if on reflection you know that
it did not lead to affliction ... it was a skillful mental
action with happy consequences, happy results, then
you should stay mentally refreshed and joyful, training
day and night in skillful mental qualities."

MN 61

The process of self-examination recommended in this passage includes the principles discussed under the first three
factors for stream-entry. You pay appropriate attention to your
own intentions and actions, and to their results, to see whether
they qualify as skillful or unskillful. If you notice that any of
your bodily or verbal actions have led to harmful results, you
approach a person of integrity and listen to his/her advice. In
this way you combine the two principles that Iti 16 and 17 recommend as the most helpful internal and external principles for
awakening: appropriate attention and friendship with admirable
people. It is no coincidence that these are precisely the two principles recommended in the discourse to the Kalamas.

Self-examination of this sort, however, shares yet another feature with the first factor for stream-entry: the need for integrity. Just as your integrity is a prerequisite for your ability to detect integrity in others, so it is a prerequisite for your ability to gauge the true nature of your intentions and the results of your actions. These are commonly the two areas of experience where people are least honest with themselves. Yet, for your practice to accord with the Dhamma, you must resist any habitual tendency to be less than totally scrupulous about them. This is why, as a preface to the above advice, the sutta shows the Buddha lecturing on the importance of truthfulness as the most essential quality for a person on the path.

Although Rahula reportedly received the above advice when he was a child, MN 19 maintains that the principles it contains can lead all the way to full Awakening. This means, of course, that they can lead to the first level of Awakening, which is stream-entry.

Stream-entry is often called the arising of the Dhamma eye. What stream-enterers see with this Dhamma eye is always expressed in the same terms: *"Whatever is subject to origination is all subject to cessation."* A passage in the Vinaya shows that the concept "all that is subject to origination" occurs in conjunction with a glimpse of what stands in opposition to "all that is subject to origination"—in other words, the Unfabricated: deathlessness.

[Immediately after attaining the Stream] Sariputta the Wanderer went to where Moggalana the Wanderer was staying. Moggalana the Wanderer saw him coming from afar and, on seeing him. said, "Your faculties are bright, my friend; your complexion pure and clear. Could it be that you have attained the Deathless?"

"Yes, my friend, I have...."

Mv I.23.5

The suttas describe the experience of the Deathless in only the sketchiest terms. What little description there is, is intended to show that the Deathless lies beyond most linguistic categories. However, there are a few indicators to show what the Deathless is not.

To begin with, it cannot be described as a state of either being nor non-being.

MahaKotthita: With the remainderless stopping and fading of the six spheres of contact [vision, hearing, smell, taste, touch, and intellection] is it the case that there is anything else?

Sariputta: Don't say that, my friend.

MahaKotthita: With the remainderless stopping and fading of the six spheres of contact, is it the case that there is not anything else?

Sariputta: Don't say that, my friend.

MahaKotthita: ...is it the case that there both is and is not anything else?

Sariputta: Don't say that, my friend.

MahaKotthita: ...is it the case that there neither is nor is not anything else?

Sariputta: Don't say that, my friend.

MahaKotthita: Being asked...if there is anything else, you say, 'Don't say that, my friend'. Being asked...if there is not anything else...if there both is and is not anything else... if there neither is nor is not anything else, you say, 'Don't say that, my friend'. Now, how is the meaning of this statement to be understood?

Sariputta: Saying...is it the case that there is anything else... is it the case that there is not anything else...is it the case that there both is and is not anything else...is it the case that there neither is nor is not anything else, one is complicating non-complication. However far the six spheres of contact go, that is how far complication goes. However far complication goes, that is how far the six spheres of contact go. With the remainderless fading and stopping of the six spheres of contact, there comes to be the stopping, the allaying of complication.

AN IV.173

Second, the dimension of the Deathless is not devoid of awareness, although the awareness here must by definition lie apart from the consciousness included in the five aggregates of fabricated experience.

"Monks, that dimension should be known where the eye (vision) stops and the perception (mental noting) of form fades. That dimension should be known where the ear stops and the perception of sound fades ... where the nose stops and the perception of aroma fades ... where the tongue stops and the perception of flavor fades ... where the body stops and the perception of tactile sensation fades ... where the intellect stops and the perception of idea/phenomenon fades: That dimension should be known."

SN XXXV.117

"Having directly known the extent of designation and the extent of the objects of designation, the extent of expression and the extent of the objects of expression, the extent of description and the extent of the objects of description, the extent of discernment and the extent of the objects of discernment, the extent to which the cycle revolves: Having directly known that, the monk is released. [To say that,] *'The monk released, having directly known that, does not see, does not know* is his opinion,' that would be mistaken.'"

DN 15

Consciousness without feature, without end
     luminous all around:
Here water, earth, fire, and wind have no footing.
Here long and short,
     coarse and fine,
     fair and foul,
     name and form
are all brought to an end.
With the stopping
of [the aggregate of] consciousness,
     each is here brought to an end.

DN 11

"Consciousness without feature, without end, luminous all around, does not partake of the solidity of earth, the liquidity of water, the radiance of fire, the windiness of wind, the divinity of devas (and so on through a list of

the various levels of godhood to) the allness of the All
(i.e., the six sense spheres)."

MN 49

"Even so, Vaccha, any form ... feeling ... perception ...
fabrication ... consciousness by which one describing the
Tathagata would describe him: That the Tathagata has
abandoned, its root destroyed, like an uprooted palm
tree, deprived of the conditions of existence, not destined for future arising. Freed from the classification of
form ... feeling ... perception ... fabrication ... consciousness, Vaccha, the Tathagata is deep, boundless,
hard to fathom, like the sea."

MN 72

"Freed, dissociated, and released from ten things,
Bahuna, the Tathagata dwells with unrestricted awareness. Which ten? Freed, dissociated, and released from
form, the Tathagata dwells with unrestricted awareness.
Freed, dissociated, and released from feeling ... from perception ... from fabrications ... from consciousness ...
from birth ... from aging ... from death ... from stress ...
Freed, dissociated, and released from defilement, the
Tathagata dwells with unrestricted awareness.

"Just as a red, blue, or white lotus born in the water and
growing in the water, rises up above the water and
stands with no water adhering to it, in the same way the
Tathagata —freed, dissociated, and released from these
ten things—dwells with unrestricted awareness."

AN X.81

These are not the words of a person who has found release
in unconsciousness.

Finally, although the Deathless is sometimes called consciousness without feature, without end, it is not to be confused
with the formless stage of concentration called the dimension of
the infinitude of consciousness. One of the main differences
between the two is that the dimension of the infinitude of consciousness is fabricated and willed (see MN 140). The element of
will, though, can be very attenuated while one is in that dimension, and only discernment at an extremely subtle level can

ferret it out. One way of testing for it is to see if there is any sense of identification with the knowing. If there is, then there is still the conceit of I-making and my-making applied to that state. Another test is to see if there is any sense that the knowing contains all things or is their source. If there is, then there is still fabrication in that state of mind, for when the Deathless is fully comprehended, the sense of unrestricted awareness as containing or acting as the source of other things is seen to be an ignorant conceit.

> "There is the case, monks, where an uninstructed run-of-the-mill person ... perceives Unbinding as Unbinding. Perceiving Unbinding as Unbinding, he conceives things about Unbinding, he conceives things in Unbinding, he conceives things coming out of Unbinding, he conceives Unbinding as 'mine,' he delights in Unbinding. Why is that? Because he has not comprehended it, I tell you....
>
> "A monk who is an arahant, devoid of mental fermentations—who has attained completion, finished the task, laid down the burden, attained the true goal, destroyed the fetters of becoming, and is released through right knowledge ... directly knows Unbinding as Unbinding. Directly knowing Unbinding as Unbinding, he does not conceive things about Unbinding, does not conceive things in Unbinding, *does not conceive things coming out of Unbinding,* does not conceive Unbinding as 'mine,' does not delight in Unbinding. Why is that? Because he has comprehended it, I tell you."
>
> MN 1

However, in line with the instructions to Gotamı and Upali, the true test of an experience of stream-entry is not in its description, but in the results it produces. The texts describe these in two ways: four factors that characterize a person who has entered the stream, and three fetters that stream-entry automatically cuts.

The four factors, according to AN X.92, are: unwavering conviction in the Buddha, unwavering conviction in the Dhamma, unwavering conviction in the Sangha, and "virtues that are appealing to the noble ones—untorn, unbroken, unspotted, unsplattered, liberating, praised by the wise, untarnished, leading to concentration." The three fetters are: self-identity views, doubt, and grasping at precepts and practices.

The two lists have their common ground in the experience of the path to stream-entry. As the path—the noble eightfold path—yields to the fruit of stream-entry, you see that although ordinary action can lead to pleasant, unpleasant, or mixed results on the level of fabricated experience, the noble eightfold path is a form of action that produces none of these results, but instead leads to the end of action (see AN IV.237). This experience cuts through any doubt about the truth of the Buddha's Awakening, thus ensuring that your conviction in the Buddha, Dhamma, and Saṅgha will not waver. Having seen the results that ordinary actions do have on the fabricated level, however, you wouldn't dare transgress the five precepts that embody the virtues appealing to the noble ones (see AN VIII.39). Still, because the Deathless is the end of action, you don't grasp at precepts and practices as the goal in and of themselves. And because you have seen the aggregates of form, feeling, perception, fabrication, and consciousness fade away in the experience of the Deathless, you would never construct an identity view around them.

Although the traditional lists of the results of stream-entry provide stringent standards for judging one's own attainment, the texts—and living Buddhist traditions today—record many instances of people who have over-estimated their attainment. Thus when you have what seems to be an attainment of this sort, you have to examine it carefully and test the mind to see if the three fetters are actually cut. And because the attainment itself is what proves or disproves the authority and authenticity of the texts, as well as the integrity of your teachers, you are ultimately left with only one guarantee of your attainment: your own integrity, which you hope has been adequately developed along the path. In keeping with the principle that the Dhamma is ultimately a quality of the mind as embodied in the entire person, the only way you can ultimately gauge the truth of the Dhamma is if you as a person are true.

Because the attainment of stream-entry can make such an enormous difference in your life, it is worth every ounce of integrity needed to attain it and to ascertain the attainment.

Then the Blessed One, picking up a little bit of dust with the tip of his fingernail, said to the monks, "What do you think, monks? Which is greater: the little bit of dust I have picked up with the tip of my fingernail, or the great earth?"

"The great earth is far greater, lord. The little bit of dust the Blessed One has picked up with the tip of his fingernail is next to nothing. It's not a hundredth, a thousandth, a one hundred-thousandth ... when compared with the great earth."

"In the same way, monks, for a disciple of the noble ones who is consummate in view, an individual who has broken through [to stream-entry], the suffering and stress totally ended and extinguished is far greater. That which remains in the state of having at most seven remaining lifetimes is next to nothing: it's not a hundredth, a thousandth, a one hundred-thousandth, when compared with the previous mass of suffering. That's how great the benefit is of breaking through to the Dhamma, monks. That's how great the benefit is of obtaining the Dhamma eye."

SN XIII.1

For a person who has been relieved of this much suffering, the question of the historical Buddha becomes irrelevant. If the genuine Deathless is not the historical Buddha's attainment, it's what a genuine Buddha would have attained. The Dhamma leading to this attainment could not have come from anyone else. As SN XXII.87 quotes the Buddha as saying, "One who sees the Dhamma sees me," i.e., the aspect of the Buddha that really matters, the aspect signaling that total freedom, the total end of suffering, is an attainable goal.

> Sole dominion over the earth,
> going to heaven,
> lordship over all worlds:
>> the fruit of Stream-entry
>> excels them.

Dhp 178

These are audacious claims, and they obviously require an approach more audacious than the historical method to test them. As the suttas indicate, nothing less than genuine integrity of character, developed through careful training and practice, will suffice. Given that "dhamma" means both teaching and quality of mind, it stands to reason that truth of character is needed to measure the truth of the teaching. Only true people can know the truth of the suttas' claims. This may seem an exclusionary or elitist thing to say, but actually it's not. The sort of education needed to master the historical method isn't open to everyone, but integrity is—if you want to develop it. The suttas say that the best things in life are available to those who are true. The only question is whether you're true enough to want to know if they're right.

Glossary

Ajaan (Thai): Teacher; mentor. Pali form: Ācariya.

Arahant: A "worthy one" or "pure one;" a person whose mind is free of defilement and thus is not destined for further rebirth. A title for the Buddha and the highest level of his noble disciples. Sanskrit form: Arhat.

Deva: Literally, "shining one." An inhabitant of the heavenly realms.

Dhamma: (1) Event; action; (2) a phenomenon in and of itself; (3) mental quality; (4) doctrine, teaching; (5) *nibbāna* (although there are passages describing nibbana as the abandoning of all dhammas). Sanskrit form: Dharma.

Jhāna: Mental absorption. A state of strong concentration focused on a single sensation or mental notion. This term is derived from the verb *jhāyati*, which means to burn with a steady, still flame. Sanskrit form: Dhyana.

Kamma: Intentional act. Sanskrit form: Karma.

Khandha: Aggregate; heap; pile. Sanskrit form: Skandha.

Nibbāna: Literally, the "unbinding" of the mind from passion, aversion, and delusion, and from the entire round of death and rebirth. As this term also denotes the extinguishing of a fire, it carries connotations of stilling, cooling, and peace. "Total nibbana" in some contexts denotes the experience of Awakening; in others, the final passing away of an arahant. Sanskrit form: Nirvana.

Samaṇa: Contemplative. Literally, a person who abandons the conventional obligations of social life in order to find a way of life more "in tune" *(sama)* with the ways of nature.

Saṁsāra: Transmigration; the process of wandering through repeated states of becoming, with their attendant death and rebirth.

Sangha: On the conventional *(sammati)* level, this term denotes the communities of Buddhist monks and nuns. On the ideal *(ariya)* level, it denotes those followers of the Buddha, lay or ordained, who have attained at least stream-entry.

Sutta: Discourse. Sanskrit form: Sutra.

Tathāgata: Literally, "one who has become authentic *(tatha-āgata),*" an epithet used in ancient India for a person who has attained the highest religious goal. In Buddhism, it usually denotes the Buddha, although occasionally it also denotes any of his arahant disciples.

Vinaya: The monastic discipline, whose rules and traditions comprise six volumes in printed text.

Abbreviations

AN	Aṅguttara Nikaya
DN	Dīgha Nikaya
Dhp	Dhammapada
Iti	Itivuttaka
MN	Majjhima Nikaya
Mv	Mahavagga
SN	Saṁyutta Nikaya
Sn	Sutta Nipata
Ud	Udana

References to DN, Iti, and MN are to discourse *(sutta).* References to Dhp are to verse. The reference to Mv is to chapter, section, and sub-section. References to other texts are to section *(saṁyutta, nipata,* or *vagga)* and discourse.

*Inquiries concerning this book
may be addressed to:*

*The Abbot
Metta Forest Monastery
PO Box 1409
Valley Center, CA 92082 USA*